The Power & Acts of Love

(The Analysis of Song of Solomon)

Pastor Lenuf

The Power & Acts of Love

Published By
HAMEO Gospel Publication Team
(www.hameo.org)

Copyright © 2010 by Lenuf
All Rights Reserved
ISBN: 978-0-557-97852-6

DEDICATED
To Jesus Christ

who makes something out of our nothingness, who is the Head and Owner of this ministry and us, and who is the inspiration behind this book. To Him are all glory, all honour, and all majesty both now and forevermore. Amen.

To My Family Members,

especially my wife, Mary E, who cooperate with God to make my home a sweet life for me.

To My 2010 Wedding Anniversary

which comes up today, October 10, 2010. May God always make my Wedding Day (October 10) a blessed and glorious day in my world. Blessed be the day forever on which the power of love was planted into my home.

&

To All Couples & Couples-to-be

whose families this book will transform.

A WORD FROM THE AUTHOR

I am most happy today, October 10, 2010, for another wedding anniversary. Here comes another day of double, double. October 10 is a day of double 10, i.e. 10-10. I was born on this date. I boldly confess that my life has been filled with double, double in every area – goodness, blessings, peace, greatness, family, and so on. Many things that happened to me are in double, double. Let me give few examples of my double, double in the area of family only. First, my birth was on double number date: 10-10, i.e. October 10. Second, I was born by Mary as a mother and I am married to another Mary as a wife. Again, I was born in October 10 and I wedded in another October 10 after many years. In childbearing, I got my children in double; I gave birth to twins. Let me reserve the rest of my doubles.

Today, October 10, 2010, is more than just being a normal day of double for me; it is a day of triple: 10-10-10. Naturally arranged, it is the unique and the best birthday date and wedding anniversary date I have ever witnessed and I will ever witness until I die (The next triple 10 date will be the next 100 years). I therefore see it necessary for me to present this book on marriage as my best gift to this day and our wedding anniversary of this year (2010). This book, The Power & Acts of Love (Marriage & Courtship Management), which has been written since 2007, is therefore sent to the publishing house today (10-10-10) to be made available to every couple and couple-to-be.

HAMEO- 4 -BOOK-LUKS

I trust this book will really be a gift to your family. It is the joy of my family, our ministry, and God himself to see every courtship successful and every family thriving well. All you need for the success of your courtship or marriage is therefore embedded in this book. Your died or dying marriage can rise up again and blossom once again. Likewise, your vibrant marriage can remain vibrant to the end. All you need to do is to practise wholeheartedly all you are instructed in this book.

All the tips and principles treated in this book are drawn from the book of Song of Solomon. This book is nothing but the Analysis of Song of Solomon. This is my product of tapping into King Solomon's great wisdom and research on the principles for successful courtship and marriage by the guidance and inspiration of the Holy Spirit. This book is therefore a book for effective management of marriage and courtship from the research of King Solomon the wisest.

To get the best from the products of the wisdom of this wisest man, King Solomon, I therefore see it necessary to establish an analysis study research for the books of King Solomon. This partnership research system between King Solomon and me is what I therefore call "Lenuf University of King Solomon (LUKS)."

Now, let us go into this book with our God, who gave all the wisdom used by Solomon for the Book of Song of Solomon and that used by me for this book, to get the best reserved in this book for our families. I wish you the best as you read.

Contents

SECTION ONE: THE SONG OF STORY OF LOVE

PART A
The Drama Helicopter View

PART B
The Application of the Drama

SECTION TWO: PRACTICAL APPLICATION IN THE HOME

PART C
Taking "Abnormality" as Uniqueness

SECTION ONE

THE SONG OF STORY OF LOVE

Part A

One

The Playwright & the Characters of the Drama

The Song of Solomon is one of the dramas we have in the Holy Bible. Being a drama, it was written by someone. Who then is the writer? The writer is nobody than the wisest man in the history of the world. This is King Solomon, the king of Israel between eleven to ten centuries before the birth of Christ. Here is the introduction of the writer from the first verse of the book:

"The song of songs, which is **Solomon's**"

King Solomon is the writer. This man is worthy to learn from always. Why? This is because he was a reservoir of God's wisdom, knowledge, and understanding. Remember that associating with such a God-fearing and God-loving wise man like this will make one wiser. He that walks with the wise will be wiser. Therefore, we must learn all he said before he died.

This King Solomon wrote three books out of the sixty-six books of the Holy Bible. They are
- Proverbs,
- Ecclesiastes, and
- Song of Solomon

We need to analyze the books one by one. If you are conversant with HAMEO publications (visit http://hameo.org/HAMEOBooks.aspx), you will know that we have analyzed Ecclesiastes and called it "The Best Businesses on Earth." If truly you have read this book, you will be able to tell me what you gained from King

Solomon.

Now, in this book named "The Power and Acts of Love," we are analyzing Song of Solomon. Here you will learn how to improve and beautify your marital home. King Solomon, the wisest, was a man that knew A to Z of how to make your family what it was meant to be. You will enjoy this book greatly since Solomon is highly worthy to learn from always. If you do not believe me, keep on reading and meditating on this book, you will tell me at the end of this book whether my statement is true or not.

Ecclesiastes has been analyzed, and this is another analysis: Song of Solomon. We can but analyze Proverbs also if God permits us and gives us the time. Therefore, watch out for the analysis of Proverbs. If you are no more a student, you must join the Lenuf University of King Solomon (LUKS) in order to tap from his wisdom. Therefore, be ready to study the analysis of Proverbs if God permits me to write it. The sketch of the analysis of Proverbs I have is in many volumes – it is a big book indeed.

Now, come back to the analysis of Song of Solomon. Since you have known the writer, you need to know the characters involved in this drama of love.

The Song of Solomon comprises six major groups of characters. They are
1. The king (This is Solomon himself) (see 1:4)

2. A beautiful Shulamite maiden (see 6:13)
3. A Shepherd a.k.a the Beloved (The maiden's spouse) (see 1:7)
4. Daughters of Jerusalem (see 1:5)
5. The Watchmen (see 3:3)
6. Friends (see 5:16)

Each of these characters plays a remarkable part in the drama. In the next chapter, I will show you the part of each character. Let us go to chapter two now.

Two

The Storyline of the Play

The book of Song of Solomon is all about mutual love between husband and wife. Solomon used this to show how God as a Husband loved him as a bride and how he loved God. Solomon was highly loved by God above all his brethren and made him a king over all the land of Israel in 1015 BC. Solomon in return demonstrated his great love for God by offering abundantly great sacrifices. 1 Kings 3:3, 4 says,

> *And Solomon* **LOVED** *the LORD, walking in the statutes of David his father: only he sacrificed and burnt incense in high places. And the king went to Gibeon to sacrifice there; for that was the great high place:* **_a thousand_** *burnt offerings did Solomon offer upon that altar. (1 Kings 3:3, 4)*

Solomon was the first person that had the record of offering one thousand burnt offerings to God. God again reciprocated this love by asking Solomon to ask whatever he wanted. God granted his request and gave him more things than he asked. As a result, Solomon became the most honourable, richest, and wisest man of his time. Even until the end of the world, no other man can be wiser than he was (1 Kings 3:12).

It is this mutual love between God (who represents the Husband) and Solomon (who represents the Wife) that Solomon transformed into drama we have in the book of Song of Solomon. He wrote this book in

1014 BC, a year after his coronation and elevation.

The story shows mutual love between a beautiful Shulamite maiden (the wife) and her spouse, the Shepherd a.k.a the Beloved. They so much loved each other that the king was unable to take the Shulamite maiden away from the Shepherd.

Right from the time the Shulamite maiden and the Shepherd were in courtship until after they have wedded as a couple, the king used every means to deprive the Shepherd of the maiden. The king tried all he could to entice or charm this woman in order to marry her but she refused due to her unquenchable love for the Shepherd. The king, who was Solomon himself, used his great fame, prospect, and wealth in order to win the love of this maiden but all his attempts were to no avail.

In the drama, the king had a group of people that ran errands for him. These are called the daughters of Jerusalem. Throughout the drama, Solomon was not found uttering any word to the maiden but he used these daughters of Jerusalem as intermediaries between him and the maiden. The daughters of Jerusalem talked and tried all they knew to make the maiden fall in love with the king but she refused. This is why the maiden rebuked then continuously for three times,

I charge you, O daughters of Jerusalem,

that ye stir not up, nor awake my love,

until he please. (8:4; also found in 2:7 and

3:5)

He rebuked them "stir not up, nor awake my love until he please." That is to say, she meant that they should stop charming and persuading her to marry the king until he (the Shepherd, her spouse-to-be) please (to marry her).

Despite all the wealth and fame of the king coupled with all the persuasions of the daughters of Jerusalem, the maiden was bent on marrying the poor despised Shepherd whom she greatly loved. As a result, they realized that "many waters cannot quench love, neither can the floods drown it: if a man would give all the substance of his house for love, it would utterly be contemned." (8:7).

There is a lot to learn in this book as we analyze it. This is why we are analyzing this book of Song of Solomon under the title of "The Power and Acts of Love." Before we continue in analyzing this book, I will like you to read the whole book of the Song of Solomon as a drama by putting each character at the front of his speech. Here it is:

THE DRAMA: SONG OF SOLOMON

1
The Song of Songs, which *is* Solomon's.

The Shulamite

2 Let him kiss me with the kisses of his mouth: for thy love *is* better than wine.

3 Because of the savour of thy good ointments thy name *is as* ointment poured forth, therefore do the virgins love thee.

The Daughters of Jerusalem

4 Draw me, we will run after thee:

The Shulamite

The king hath brought me into his chambers:

The Daughters of Jerusalem

We will be glad and rejoice in thee, we will remember thy love more than wine: the upright love thee.

The Shulamite

5 I *am* black, but comely, O ye daughters of Jerusalem, as the tents of Kedar, as the curtains of Solomon.

6 Look not upon me, because I *am* black, because the sun hath looked upon me: my mother's children were angry with me; they made me the keeper of the vineyards; *but* mine own vineyard have I not kept.

The Shulamite *(To Her Beloved)*

7 Tell me, O thou whom my soul loveth, where thou feedest, where thou makest *thy flock* to rest at noon: for why should I be as one that turneth aside by the flocks of thy companions?

The Beloved

8 If thou know not, O thou fairest among women, go thy way forth by the footsteps of the flock, and feed thy kids beside the shepherds' tents.

9 I have compared thee, O my love, to a company of horses in Pharaoh's chariots.

10 Thy cheeks are comely with rows *of jewels*, thy neck with chains *of gold*.

The Daughters of Jerusalem

11 We will make thee borders of gold with studs of silver.

The Shulamite

12 While the king *sitteth* at his table, my spikenard sendeth forth the smell thereof.

13 A bundle of myrrh *is* my well beloved unto me; he shall lie all night betwixt my breasts.

14 My beloved *is* unto me *as* a cluster of camphire in the vineyards of Engedi.

The Beloved

15 Behold, thou *art* fair, my love; behold, thou *art* fair; thou *hast* doves' eyes.

The Shulamite

16 Behold, thou *art* fair, my beloved, yea, pleasant: also our bed *is* green.

17 The beams of our house *are* cedar, *and* our rafters of fir.

The Beloved

2 I *am* the rose of Sharon, *and* the lily of the valleys.

2 As the lily among thorns, so *is* my love among the daughters.

The Shulamite

3 As the apple tree among the trees of the wood, so *is* my beloved among the sons. I sat down under his shadow with great delight, and his fruit *was* sweet to my taste.

The Shulamite *(To the Daughters of Jerusalem)*

> 4 He brought me to the banqueting house, and his banner over me *was* love.
>
> 5 Stay me with flagons, comfort me with apples: for I *am* sick of love.
>
> 6 His left hand *is* under my head, and his right hand doth embrace me.
>
> 7 I charge you, O ye daughters of Jerusalem, by the roes, and by the hinds of the field, that ye stir not up, nor awake *my* love, till he please.

The Shulamite

> 8 The voice of my beloved! behold, he cometh leaping upon the mountains, skipping upon the hills.
>
> 9 My beloved is like a roe or a young hart: behold, he standeth behind our wall, he looketh forth at the windows, shewing himself through the lattice.

10 My beloved spake, and said unto me, Rise up, my love, my fair one, and come away.

11 For, lo, the winter is past, the rain is over *and* gone;

12 The flowers appear on the earth; the time of the singing *of birds* is come, and the voice of the turtle is heard in our land;

13 The fig tree putteth forth her green figs, and the vines *with* the tender grape give a *good* smell. Arise, my love, my fair one, and come away.

14 O my dove, *that art* in the clefts of the rock, in the secret *places* of the stairs, let me see thy countenance, let me hear thy voice; for sweet *is* thy voice, and thy countenance *is* comely.

15 Take us the foxes, the little foxes, that spoil the vines: for our vines *have* tender grapes.

16 My beloved *is* mine, and I *am* his: he feedeth among the lilies.

The Beloved *(To her Beloved)*

17 Until the day break, and the shadows flee away, turn, my beloved, and be thou like a roe or a young hart upon the mountains of Bether.

The Shulamite

3 By night on my bed I sought him whom my soul loveth: I sought him, but I found him not.

2 I will rise now, and go about the city in the streets, and in the broad ways I will seek him whom my soul loveth: I sought him, but I found him not.

3 The watchmen that go about the city found me: *to whom I said*, Saw ye him whom my soul loveth?

4 *It was* but a little that I passed from them, but I found him whom my soul loveth: I held him, and would not let him go, until I had brought him into my mother's house, and into he chamber of her that conceived me.

5 I charge you, O ye daughters of Jerusalem, by the roes, and by the hinds of the field, that ye stir not up, nor awake *my* love, till he please.

6 Who *is* this that cometh out of the wilderness like pillars of smoke, perfumed with myrrh and frankincense, with all powders of the merchant?

7 Behold his bed, which *is* Solomon's; threescore valiant men *are* about it, of the valiant of Israel.

8 They all hold swords, *being* expert in war: everyman *hath* his sword upon his thigh because of fear in the night.

9 King Solomon made himself a chariot of the wood of Lebanon.

10 He made the pillars thereof *of* silver, the bottom thereof *of* gold, the covering of it *of* purple, the midst thereof being paved *with* love, for the daughters of Jerusalem.

11 Go forth, O ye daughters of Zion, and behold king Solomon with the crown wherewith his mother crowned him in the day of his espousals, and in the day of the gladness of his heart.

The Beloved

4 Behold, thou *art* fair, my love; behold, thou *art* fair; thou *hast* doves' eyes within thy locks: thy hair *is* as a flock of goats, that appear from mount Gilead.

2 Thy teeth *are* like a flock *of sheep that are even* shorn, which came up from the washing; whereof every one bear twins, and none *is* barren among them.

3 Thy lips *are* like a thread of scarlet, and thy speech *is* comely: thy temples *are* like a piece of a pomegranate within thy locks.

4 Thy neck *is* like the tower of David builded for an armoury, whereon there hang a thousand bucklers, all shields of mighty men.

5 Thy two breasts *are* like two young roes that are twins, which feed among the lilies.

6 Until the day break, and the shadows flee away, I will get me to the mountain of myrrh, and to the hill of frankincense.

7 Thou *art* all fair, my love; *there is* no spot in thee.

8 Come with me from Lebanon, *my* spouse, with me from Lebanon: look from the top of Amana, from the top of Shenir and Hermon, from the lions' dens, from the mountains of the leopards.

9 Thou hast ravished my heart, my sister, *my* spouse; thou hast ravished my heart with one of thine eyes, with one chain of thy neck.

10 How fair is thy love, my sister, *my* spouse! how much better is thy love than wine! and the smell of thine ointments than all spices!

11 Thy lips, O *my* spouse, drop *as* the honeycomb: honey and milk *are* under thy tongue; and the smell of thy

garments *is* like the smell of Lebanon.

12 A garden inclosed *is* my sister, *my* spouse; a spring shut up, a fountain sealed.

13 Thy plants *are* an orchard of pomegranates, with pleasant fruits; camphire, with spikenard,

14 Spikenard and saffron; calamus and cinnamon, with all trees of frankincense; myrrh and aloes, with all the chief spices:

15 A fountain of gardens, a well of living waters, and streams from Lebanon.

The Shulamite

16 Awake, O north wind; and come, thou south; blow upon my garden, *that* the spices thereof may flow out. Let my beloved come into his garden, and eat his pleasant fruits.

The Beloved

5 I am come into my garden, my sister, *my* spouse: I have gathered my myrrh with my spice; I have eaten my honey comb with my honey; I have drunk my wine with my milk: eat, O friends; drink, yea, drink abundantly, O beloved.

The Shulamite

2 I sleep, but my heart waketh: *it is* the voice of my beloved that knocketh, *saying*, Open to me, my sister, my love, my dove, my undefiled: for my head is filled with dew, *and* my locks with the drops of the night.

3 I have put off my coat; how shall I put it on? I have washed my feet; how shall I defile them?

4 My beloved put in his hand by the hole *of the door*, and my bowels were moved for him.

5 I rose up to open to my beloved; and my hands dropped *with* myrrh, and my fingers *with* sweet smelling myrrh, upon the handles of the lock.

6 I opened to my beloved; but my beloved had withdrawn himself, *and* was gone: my soul failed when he spake: I sought him, but I could not find him; I called him, but he gave me no answer.

7 The watchmen that went about the city found me, they smote me, they wounded me; the keepers of the walls took away my veil from me.

8 I charge you, O daughters of Jerusalem, if ye find my beloved, that ye tell him, that I *am* sick of love.

The Daughters of Jerusalem

9 What *is* thy beloved more than *another* beloved, O thou fairest among women? what *is* thy beloved more than *another* beloved, that thou dost so charge us?

The Shulamite

10 My beloved *is* white and ruddy, the chiefest among ten thousand.

11 His head *is as* the most fine gold, his locks *are* bushy, *and* black as a raven.

12 His eyes *are* as *the eyes* of doves by the rivers of waters, washed with milk, *and* fitly set.

13 His cheeks *are* as a bed of spices, *as* sweet flowers: his lips *like* lilies, dropping sweet smelling myrrh.

14 His hands *are as* gold rings set with the beryl: his belly *is as* bright ivory overlaid *with* sapphires.

15 His legs *are as* pillars of marble, set upon sockets of fine gold: his countenance *is* as Lebanon, excellent as the cedars.

16 His mouth *is* most sweet: yea, he *is* altogether lovely. This *is* my beloved, and this *is* my friend, O daughters of Jerusalem.

The Daughters of Jerusalem

6 Whither is thy beloved gone, O thou fairest among women? whither is thy beloved turned aside? that we may seek him with thee.

The Shulamite

2 My beloved is gone down into his garden, to the beds of spices, to feed in the gardens, and to gather lilies.

3 I *am* my beloved's, and my beloved *is* mine: he feedeth among the lilies.

The Beloved

4 Thou *art* beautiful, O my love, as Tirzah, comely as Jerusalem, terrible as *an army* with banners.

5 Turn away thine eyes from me, for they have overcome me: thy hair *is* as a flock of goats that appear from Gilead.

6 Thy teeth *are* as a flock of sheep which go up from the washing, whereof every one beareth twins, and *there is* not one barren among them.

7 As a piece of a pomegranate *are* thy temples within thy locks.

8 There are threescore queens, and fourscore concubines, and virgins without number.

9 My dove, my undefiled is *but* one; she *is* the *only* one of her mother, she *is* the choice *one* of her that bare her. The daughters saw her, and blessed her; *yea,* the queens and the concubines, and they praised her.

10 Who *is* she *that* looketh forth as the morning, fair as the moon, clear as the sun, *and* terrible as *an army* with banners?

The Shulamite

11 I went down into the garden of nuts to see the fruits of the valley, *and* to see whether the vine flourished, *and* the pomegranates budded.

12 Or ever I was aware, my soul made me *like* the chariots of Amminadib.

The Beloved and His Friends

13 Return, return, O Shulamite; return, return, that we may look upon thee. What will ye see in the Shulamite? As it were the company of two armies.

The Beloved

7 How beautiful are thy feet with shoes, O prince's daughter! the joints of thy thighs *are* like jewels, the work of the hands of a cunning workman.

2 Thy navel *is like* a round goblet, *which* wanteth not liquor: thy belly *is like* an heap of wheat set about with lilies.

3 Thy two breasts *are* like two young roes *that are* twins.

4 Thy neck *is* as a tower of ivory; thine eyes *like* the fish pools in Heshbon, by the gate of Bathrabbim: thy nose *is* as the tower of Lebanon which looketh toward Damascus.

5 Thine head upon thee *is* like Carmel, and the hair of thine head like purple; the king *is* held in the galleries.

6 How fair and how pleasant art thou, O love, for delights!

7 This thy stature is like to a palm tree, and thy breasts to clusters *of grapes*.

8 I said, I will go up to the palm tree, I will take hold of the boughs thereof: now also thy breasts shall be as clusters of the vine, and the smell of thy nose like apples;

9 And the roof of thy mouth like the best wine for my beloved, that goeth *down* sweetly, causing the lips of those that are asleep to speak.

The Shulamite

10 I *am* my beloved's, and his desire *is* toward me.

11 Come, my beloved, let us go forth into the field; let us lodge in the villages.

12 Let us get up early to the vineyards; let us see if the vine flourish, *whether* the tender grape appear, *and* the pomegranates bud forth: there will I give thee my loves.

13 The mandrakes give a smell, and at our gates *are* all manner of pleasant *fruits*, new and old, *which* I have laid up for thee, O my beloved.

The Shulamite

8 O that thou *wert* as my brother, that sucked the breasts of my mother! *when* I should find thee without, I would kiss thee; yea, I should not be despised.

2 I would lead thee, *and* bring thee into my mother's house, *who* would instruct me: I would cause thee to drink of spiced wine of the juice of my pomegranate.

The Shulamite *(To the Daughters of Jerusalem)*

3 His left hand *should be* under my head, and his right hand should embrace me.

4 I charge you, O daughters of Jerusalem, that ye stir not up, nor awake *my* love, until he please.

An Observer *(Probably a Relative)*

> 5 Who *is* this that cometh up from the wilderness, leaning upon her beloved?

The Beloved

> I raised thee up under the apple tree: there thy mother brought thee forth: there she brought thee forth *that* bare thee.

The Shulamite *(To Her Beloved)*

> 6 Set me as a seal upon thine heart, as a seal upon thine arm: for love *is* strong as death; jealousy *is* cruel as the grave: the coals thereof *are* coals of fire, *which hath a* most vehement flame.
>
> 7 Many waters cannot quench love, neither can the floods drown it: if *a* man would give all the substance of his house for love, it would utterly be contemned.

The Beloved and His Friends

8 We have a little sister, and she hath no breasts: what shall we do for our sister in the day when she shall be spoken for?

9 If she *be* a wall, we will build upon her a palace of silver: and if she *be* a door, we will in close her with boards of cedar.

The Shulamite

10 I *am* a wall, and my breasts like towers: then was I in his eyes as one that found favour.

11 Solomon had a vineyard at Baalhamon; he let out the vineyard unto keepers; every one for the fruit thereof was to bring a thousand *pieces* of silver.

The Shulamite *(To Solomon)*

12 My vineyard, which *is* mine, *is* before me: thou, O Solomon, *must have* a thousand, and those that keep the fruit thereof two hundred.

The Beloved

> 13 Thou that dwellest in the gardens, the companions hearken to thy voice: cause me to hear *it*.

The Shulamite

> 14 Make haste, my beloved, and be thou like to a roe or to a young hart upon the mountains of spices.

<u>Part B</u>

THE APPLICATION OF THE DRAMA

Three

A Mystery: Christ & the Church

This drama is typical of the relationship between Christ and the church. Remember that Christ is the Husband while the church is His bride or wife. Ephesians 5:23 affirms, "For the husband is the head of the wife, <u>even as Christ is the head of the church</u>: he is the savior of the body."

The husband-wife relationship between Christ and the church is a great mystery. This is why Ephesians 5:32 says,

> *This is a great mystery: but I speak concerning Christ and the church. (Ephesians 5:32)*

This drama unveils to us, on one side, the mystery of mutual love and husband-wife relationship between Christ and the church. Therefore, this drama has a right application in the kingdom of God to show how Christ loves Christians (the church) and how Christians show love and reverence for Christ.

Let me show you some words or expressions that point to Christ and the church.

2:1 refers to Christ: "I am the <u>Rose of Sharon</u>, and the <u>Lily of the valleys</u>."

In verse 4:7, Christ describes the beauty of holiness of the church by saying, "Thou art all fair, my love, <u>there is no spot in thee</u>." In 5:2, Christ calls the church, "My undefiled."

In 5:10, the church describes the holiness and superiority of Christ, "My beloved is white and ruddy, the chiefest among ten thousand." She further confesses Christ's lordship over her, "I am my beloved's, and his desire is toward me." (7:10)

In summary, the whole drama can be broken down as the interaction between Christ and the church. Here is the breakdown:

Chapter 1

1-4   *Church's love unto Christ*
5-6   *The Church confesses her deformity*
7   *She prays to be directed to His flock*
8   *Christ directs her to the shepherds' tents*
9-10   *Christ shows His love to her*
11   *He gives her gracious promises*
12-17   *The church and Christ congratulate one another*

Chapter 2

1-7   *The mutual love of Christ and His church*
8-9   *The hope of the church*
10-13   *The calling of the church*
14-15   *Christ's care of the church*
16-17   *The profession of the church*

Chapter 3

Chapter 4

Chapter 5

Chapter 6

Chapter 7

Chapter 8

Four

A Demand: You & Your Spouse

It is demanded that the same love that exists between Christ and the church should exist between you and your spouse. Let us hear from Ephesians 5:24, 25, 32, and 33:

> *Therefore as the church is subject to Christ, so let the wives be to their own husbands in every thing. Husbands, love your wives, even as Christ also loved the church, and gave himself for it; This is a great mystery: but I speak concerning Christ and the church. Nevertheless let every one of you in particular so love his wife even as himself; and the wife see that she reverence her husband.*

The strong unquenchable love between Christ and the church should be seen in your family. This is why we are analyzing this book of Song of Solomon. The drama in the book purely shows how you and your spouse should relate. This is God's demand for your family. This is why God made this drama to be written for your learning according to Romans 15:4:

> *For whatsoever things were written aforetime were written for our learning, that we through patience and comfort of the scriptures might have hope.*

It was not only written down in the Bible for you

to read but God has also inspired HAMEO to analyze it further for your practical use in your family. The practical analysis of this drama that will be beneficial to your family is treated in section two of this book. Without wasting time, let us launch into the section two of this book now!

SECTION TWO

PRACTICAL APPLICATION

IN THE

HOME

Part C

TAKING "ABNORMALITY" AS UNIQUENESS

Five

Take Your Spouse as He/She is

The beautiful Shulamite maiden was a black person among all other white people around her. Hear what she said, "I am BLACK, but comely, O ye daughters of Jerusalem, as the tents of Kedar, as the curtains of Solomon" (1:5).

Being black among all other whites people, some people will see her or call her abnormal woman. However, be informed that she was not abnormal but unique. What is uniqueness? Uniqueness is the quality of being different from others, while abnormality is the state that deviates from normal pattern.

The question to answer is "What is the single normal human pattern established by God?" Tell me if you know. God did not create man in a single pattern but in different patterns – some are white, some are red, and some are black; some are tall, some are moderate in height while some are short; some have small eyeballs while some have big; some have gaps in their teeth while some have not; some have big heads while some have small ones; some stammer while some are not; some speak very fast while some speak slowly; and so on.

God created every person uniquely from his or her neighbours. Therefore, there is nothing like abnormality in any human being but that thing we see as abnormality in him or her is his or her

uniqueness. This is what I call <u>Lenuf's Doctrine of</u> <u>Human Uniqueness.</u>

The Shulamite maiden therefore warns,

> *Look not upon me, because I am black,*
>
> *because the sun hath looked upon me: my*
>
> *mother's children were angry with me;*
>
> *they made me the keeper of the vineyards;*
>
> *but mine own vineyard have I not kept.*
>
> *(1:6)*

She warned her spouse not to look down on her because she was darker than others around. New International Version puts the verse above this way: "Do not stare at me because I am black." Though her darkness was artificially induced by excessive exposure to sun's heat, her darkness should not be taken as "abnormality but as her uniqueness."

It is the same view expected of you. Take your spouse as he or she is. Never take any special feature in his/her body or character as abnormality but take it as his or her uniqueness among other existing members of the opposite sex.

Do you know that so many married individuals

are not content with their spouses? So also, many unmarried young men and women complain about their fiancées and fiancés respectively. They complain all the time: "My spouse is too short, too dark, too slim, or slender. He (she) is this and that. Had I thought it well, I would not have married him (or her). I am tired of this marriage (courtship). What an abnormal husband (wife) I married (or about to marry)!"

My friend, be informed that he or she is not abnormal but is the unique person to marry. You see your spouse's unique features as "abnormality" because your heart gives you abnormal judgement and evaluation.

Do not forget that beauty is in the eyes of the beholder. **It is the judgement, evaluation, and reference you give in your heart that your eyes will see. While evaluating the most beautiful spouse, set all the features of your spouse as a reference point for ascribing highest beauty.** For instance, there is no feature I cherish like those I find in my wife. I prayed to God to give me a wife and God showed her to me. Since that time, I set her as a reference point for evaluating the most beautiful.

The best height I like from any female is hers. I make her completion to be the best. I make the arrangement of her teeth as the best arrangement. Until today, I have not seen any abnormality in my wife but all I see in her is uniqueness. My wife is so unique to me because I count all her special or uncommon features not as **"abnormal"** features but as **"above normal"** (exceptional) and unique features.

So also your spouse does not have any abnormality but uniqueness ("above normal" features) in every area – from head to toe. Why? This is because <u>**any feature in any person that is not common in many people is a unique feature of that person. There is nothing like abnormality in any human being. All things we see as "abnormal" features in anybody are his or her "above normal" and exceptional features.**</u> Again, here comes in *Lenuf's Doctrine of Human Uniqueness*. In this doctrine, the first two letters "ab" prefix in abnormal are abbreviated form of above. Every feature we see in any human as abnormal is his or her "above normal" features. "Above normal" means exceptional. What is exceptional then? Exceptional means, "Surpassing what is common or usual or expected." It also means, "Far beyond what is usual in magnitude or degree." All the features we see as abnormal features in a person are therefore unique, exceptional, and above normal features of that person.

Therefore, a spouse with a big eyeball is unique among others. A spouse with big head is unique among others. A very dark spouse is unique among others. A very slender spouse is unique among others. In summary, **anything you see as odd feature in your spouse is his or her uniqueness.**

Do you know that any artificially induced feature is a unique feature? That deformity in your spouse is his or her uniqueness. Do you know that if a car were manufactured today with two wheels only, many people including you would like to buy it in preference of the other existing cars with four or more wheels? Why? This is because this car is unique to all other existing cars. Do you know that this car is deformed? Normally, a car should have at least four wheels but this is only having two. Nevertheless, does anybody regard this deformity as "abnormality"? No! Everybody regards this deformity of having only two wheels as a unique characteristic of the car. This is why the whole world would be aspiring to buy such a car.

Therefore, do not look down on your spouse neither do you despise him or her because of his or her deformity. Take your spouse as he or she is. The Shulamite says,

Look not upon me, because I am black...

Your spouse can never be totally beautiful or handsome in your sight until you have turned his or her special features (that you call or see as abnormalities) to uniqueness. According to computer, term WYSIWYG, it is "What You See Is What You Get." If you see those features as abnormality, he or she will be ugly in your sight and be irritating to you. On the other hand, if you see those features as his or her uniqueness, he or she will be tower of most excellent beauty in your sight.

What makes many people to lust after or prefer other people's spouses to theirs is that they use the features those other spouses possess as a yardstick and reference point for measuring beauty. Since their spouses do no possess those features, they see them as ugly people.

I told you earlier that my wife's features are the yardstick and reference point that I use to measure how beautiful all other females are. Those people that have one or more of her features are more beautiful in my sight than others. **My wife is so beautiful and unique in my sight because there is no**

other female that is exactly like her. This is why I cannot do without her. In fact, she is my "life" that must not be taken from me. This is how you should take your spouse. Take him or her as he or she is.

Go back and change your orientation about your spouse; he or she is so unique than to be judged as an abnormal spouse. Behave like the Beloved (the Shulamite's spouse) who did not regard the darkness of the Shulamite's complexion as abnormality but as uniqueness. Hear the comment of the Beloved in response to the Shulamite speech in verse 6 above:

> *If thou know not, O **thou fairest among women**, go thy way forth by the footsteps of the flock, and feed thy kids beside the shepherds' tents. **I have compared thee, O my love**, to a company of horses in Pharaoh's chariots. **Thy cheeks are comely** with rows of jewels, thy neck with chains of gold. (1:8-10)*

Despite her artificially tarnished dark skin, her spouse, the Beloved, saw her as the "fairest among women" in the world. He saw her as the "fairest" (the most beautiful). He also said, "I have compared thee..."

What did he see? After the comparison, he saw her as the "fairest" because of her unique dark skin which other women around did not have. When he looked at his cheek, he said, "Thy cheeks are comely." He saw comeliness (i.e. attractiveness) in the cheeks.

Go back and change your orientation concerning your spouse. He or she is so unique because he or she possesses some qualities or features that cannot be seen or are not common to see in other members of the same sex of his or hers. These qualities and features are his or her uniqueness; they are not abnormality at all. Let me ask you a question. Who is the most beautiful or handsome person you have ever seen? By now, your answer should be your spouse.

Never look down on your spouse just because he or she is this or that. Take him or her as the tower of highest beauty. As I said earlier, do not forget that beauty is in the eyes of the beholder. **It is the judgement, evaluation, and reference you give in your heart that your eye will see.** Therefore, while evaluating the most beautiful spouse, set all the features of your spouse as a reference point and a yardstick for measuring beauty. Finally, take your spouse, fiancé, or fiancée as he or she is. He or she is unique. "If you love me, love my pet!" Therefore, love all the physical features of your spouse.

<u>Six</u>

Develop Your Spouse to Your Taste

Recently, I was with an elderly bachelor who had earlier discussed his fiancée with me. This time that we met again, I asked him about how far he had gone in preparation for his marriage. He told me that he was no more interested in that fiancée. I asked "Why and what happened?" He said that she was careless and wasteful.

I replied him, "If you are always troubled by the carelessness and some other little or trivial abnormal deeds of your fiancée you will never find a wife to marry. If you go for another fiancée, you will also see some little abnormal deeds in her life. Don't be scared, you are the one that will develop your spouse to your taste."

Every man is not very complete in the sight of his fiancée, so also every woman is not very complete before her fiancé. What matter is that when they come together in marriage as husband and wife, it is now the duty of each one of them to develop his or her spouse to his or her taste.

Let me illustrate this fact further by continuing analyzing the Song of Solomon. This is all about naïve state of the Shulamite before she married the Beloved.

Her underdeveloped, inexperienced and naïve life was metaphorically term as "she hath no breasts." The passage read thus:

> *We have a little sister, and she hath no breasts: what shall we do for our sister in the day when she shall be spoken for?*
> *(8:8)*

The question is "what shall we do for our sister"? Remember that she "hath no breasts." If you were her fiancé and discovered that she had no breasts, what would you do? Would you still marry her?"

Remember that statement "she hath no breasts" is a metaphor to depict incompleteness, inexperience, ignorance, and naïve behaviours. Maybe she did not know how to cook well; perhaps she did not know how to wash clothes; perhaps she cannot read and write; probably she could not express herself in a simple and correct official language you speak. Perhaps she was too extravagant in spending. If you were her fiancé, would you still go ahead to marry her?

The verse 8 above asks, "What shall we do for our sister in the day when she shall be spoken for?" The question came to the Beloved, her fiancé. What did he do? In verse 9, the Beloved answered discreetly,

If she be a wall, we will build upon her a palace of silver: and if she be a door, we will in close her with boards of cedar.

Please, can you help me to clap for him? He answered courageously that he would develop her to his taste no matter how useless or naïve she may be. This is a great lesson for you. He said that if she were an ordinary "wall," he would develop her to become a palace, not an ordinary palace, but "a palace of silver." Again, he said that if she were "a door," he would develop her, decorate her, and "enclose her with boards of cedar."

What a wonderful husband is this Beloved! This is what is expected of you. I once resolved that if I married a "useless" wife, I would develop her to be the most useful wife in the world. Why? This is because of the power of love I would have for her. How did the Beloved do it? Let's read verse five:

Who is this that cometh up from the wilderness, leaning upon her beloved? I raised thee up under the apple tree: there thy mother brought thee forth: there she brought thee forth that bare thee.

According to this verse, the Beloved raised her "up under the apple tree," where she was born. This apple tree signifies a low class. Let us assume she was born in a village and she grew up in the village with all sorts of naïve lifestyles of village people. She was born in the village and remained in the village until the Beloved met her. This is why he said in the verse 5 above that he raised her up from where she was born. Despite her low estate, the Beloved developed her.

Despite she was a naïve person, the Beloved still desired to marry her. He later developed her to a queen. When the daughters of Jerusalem saw her, they saw her new beauty and remarked, "O thou fairest among women." You too can develop your "useless" spouse to useful spouse.

When the Shulamite observed all the development she got from the Beloved, from an unknown person to a fairest person, from an inexperienced woman to a highly experienced woman, from being a maiden to being a happy loved wife, she concluded that it was nothing but a favour. In verse 10 of that our chapter eight, she confessed,

I am a wall, and my breasts like towers:

*then was I in his <u>eyes as one that</u> <u>**found**</u>*

*<u>**favour**</u>.*

It is indeed true that she found favour. She found favour because her spouse developed her to his taste. As a result, this woman saw the Beloved as her own taste. She said,

I sat down under his shadow with great delight, and his fruit was sweet to MY TASTE. (2:3b)

So also, it is today. **If you develop your spouse to your taste, you will consequently become the taste of your spouse. The more you develop your spouse, the more love he or she will have for you.** Take pain to develop your spouse to your taste. Stop complaining that your wife does not know how to cook. Develop her in the area of cooking. If you know how to cook better, teach her. You can do better to send her to catering class or school.

Stop complaining that my husband or my wife does not know how to read, write, and speak English or French fluently. Can you teach him or her? Do you not know that you can teach him or her better than any other teacher can do? Furthermore, you can develop him or her further, by sending him or her to higher school to further his or her education. Don't you know that a primary school certificate wife can become a professor if you train her further? Just develop your spouse to your taste.

It is observed that many bachelors and unmarried women prefer to go into endogamy than to marry according to the leading of God. Their complaint is that how can one marry to someone that is not of the same tribe or ethnic group. They prefer to marry the persons that will speak the same dialects with them. Well, that's good! However, that should not make you to kick at God's will. What to do is to marry that person that God wants you to marry and then teach him or her language or dialect of yours. Develop him or her to your taste.

Is he or she extravagant in spending, lazy, talking too much, coming home late in the night, not humble, not respectful and not courteous enough etc, you can develop him or her to your taste. **<u>You are the driver of your family. Any direction or development that cannot be carried out physically can be carried out in prayers.</u>**

I am still learning. My wife trains and develops me to her taste; I also develop her to my taste. When I see her development, I am happy. Likewise, when she sees my development and changes, she is happy.

How do you want your spouse-to-be? Go and

draw the picture of what you want your spouse-to-be. Go and write down all the qualities you want him or her to possess. This then serves as your family budget. Then go further to implement it through training of love.

One of the easiest things to do is developing your spouse by yourself. This type of development or training is carried out like a play of love. It will be as if two children are playing. For instance, as a husband, you can tell your wife, "I want to show you that I am a cook and caterer by nature. This evening, I will be the cook while you watch me. As I cook, just be watching my cooking method and, at the same time, be entertaining me with songs of love." I think your wife can never forget that evening throughout her lifetime. This is a play of love, it's more than the one you play on bed; yet you've achieved your aim of teaching her how to cook what she did know before.

Every development and training you want to give to your spouse should be wrapped with love and play of love without insulting him or her. Be patient and gentle with his or her slow rate of development. If he or she is "a wall," "build upon her a palace of silver." If he or she is "a door," "enclose her with boards of cedar." As you do this, your spouse will finally become your taste. Raise him or her from "under the apple tree" where you meet him or her.

Never allow him or her to remain breastless but develop and build his or her breasts to protrude to your taste. This is the duty of love to do.

> *We have a little sister, and she hath no breasts: what shall we do for our sister in the day when she shall be spoken for? If she be a wall, we will build upon her a palace of silver: and if she be a door, we will in close her with boards of cedar. (8:8, 9)*

Seven

Value & Prefer Your Spouse to Others

You have learnt how to take all the assumed, alleged, so-called, and wrongly impressed "abnormalities" of your spouse as his or her uniqueness by (1) taking him or her as he or she is; (2) developing him or her to your desired taste. In addition to these two acts, value your spouse than and prefer him or her to any other person in the world.

Value every feature in your spouse's body as the best feature to be seen in human body. Value the nature, shape, and size of his or her head, hair, eyes, hands, legs, and other parts than those of other people. Value his or her accent than those of others. Value the ways he or she talks, walks, does every other thing than those of other people. In summary, value him or her as the unique person to live with and marry in this world. Prefer your spouse to anyone you have ever seen and you will ever see in this world.

Well, all I have said so far is neither just a man's theory nor a hypothesis but it is a practical lifestyle of marriage. All I said so far is inferred from the book of Song of Solomon we have been analyzing. You need to see and hear it by yourself from the same book.

One day the Shulamite was seriously looking for her spouse, the Beloved, in the city on a certain night. "The watchmen that went about the city found" her and "smote," "wounded" and disciplined her for moving about in the night (See 5:6,7). The discipline did not quench the power of love she had to locate her spouse. She went further searching and searching. She said, "I sought him, but I could not find him; I called him, but he gave me no answer" (5:6b). As she went further, she came across the daughters of Jerusalem and said to them;

I charge you, O daughters of Jerusalem, if

ye find my beloved, that ye tell him, that I

am sick of love. (5:8)

When the daughters of Jerusalem, who had been trying to convince her and win her to marry their master, Solomon, heard that, they laughed her to scorn. They replied,

What is thy beloved more than another

beloved, O thou fairest among women?

what is thy beloved more than another

beloved, that thou dost so charge us? (5:9)

They were discouraging and dissuading her from loving the Beloved. They were asking her what she saw in the useless shepherd. They were trying to tell her "We told you to marry the most Very Important Person (VIP) all over the world known as King Solomon, the greatest, wisest, and richest man and king, but you refused. You prefer to marry that nonentity and useless man of our time. Tell us, what do you see in him? Why do you prefer to abandon the richest man to marry an ordinary shepherd who is wretched and smelling of sheep?"

They questioned her repeatedly, "What is thy beloved more than another beloved, O thou fairest among women." They tried to convince her that she was too beautiful and fair to marry that local man. They were trying to tell her, "Your stuff is above that man. That shepherd is not your stuff at all. Please, be wise!"

They went further to tell her that she was asking them a foolish and silly question by asking them about her poor beloved. This is what they meant by asking, "What is thy beloved more than another beloved, <u>that thou dost so charge us?</u>"

I thank God for the Shulamite. She answered them wisely and proved to them that her beloved was far, far better than any other person in the world was. She replied,

> *My beloved is <u>white</u> and <u>ruddy</u>, the*
>
> *<u>chiefest</u> among ten thousand. <u>His head</u> is*
>
> *as the most fine gold, <u>his locks</u> are bushy,*
>
> *and black as a raven. <u>His eyes</u> are as the*
>
> *eyes of doves by the rivers of waters,*

washed with milk, and fitly set. His

cheeks are as a bed of spices, as sweet

flowers: his lips like lilies, dropping sweet

smelling myrrh. His hands are as gold

rings set with the beryl: his belly is as

bright ivory overlaid with sapphires. His

legs are as pillars of marble, set upon

sockets of fine gold: his countenance is as

Lebanon, excellent as the cedars. His

mouth is most sweet: yea, he is

ALTOGETHER LOVELY. This is my

beloved, and this is my friend, O

daughters of Jerusalem. (5:10-16)

Yes, you have heard the answer of a woman of discretion. She commenced by showing them that she preferred her spouse to other men in the world, Solomon inclusive. She said,

*My beloved is ... the **CHIEFEST** among*

ten thousand.

She proved to them that her beloved was

preferred to ten thousand men combined together. This is a lesson for you. Prefer your spouse, fiancé, or fiancée to the world combined.

She proceeded to prove to them why her beloved is "the chiefest among ten thousand." She listed the priceless and invaluable qualities and features of her beloved. She said, "My beloved is <u>white and ruddy</u>," i.e. very attractive. After this statement, she listed the features and beauty of the parts of her beloved's body – from head to leg. She described "his head," "his locks" (i.e. his hair), "his eyes," "his cheeks," "his lips," "his hands," "his belly," "his legs," "his countenance" (i.e. his face or facial appearance), and "his mouth."

About "his head," she said that it was as fine as "fine gold." About "his locks" (his hairs), she said that it was attractively black and much. She described "his eyes" as the best eyes that she had ever seen. According to her, it is "as the eyes of doves" that was "washed with milk" and that it was "fitly set" than every other eyes. What a perfect description! She gave a perfect description of the other parts of his body.

She said that "his lips" were as beautiful as "lilies." Besides, the lips were constantly "dropping sweet smelling myrrh." What she meant is that his lips were very attractive that she cannot afford to miss kissing the lips always. She proved to them that Solomon does not have such lips. These were the lips she would like to kiss in the morning before leaving for work and kiss in the night before sleeping. This is why she said,

> *Let him kiss me with the kisses of HIS*
>
> *MOUTH: for thy love is better than wine.*
>
> *(1:2)*

She went further to describe "his mouth" as the "most sweet" mouth that she had ever seen. She preferred to hear the speech of this mouth always. She was never comfortable whenever her husband was absent. This was why she went about seeking for him to hear his voice once again. O, this is power of love indeed. If I were the person marrying that your spouse, this is how I would so much desire to be with him or her and hear his or her best voice always.

She later added, "He is altogether lovely." She told them that he was not almost but completely and "altogether lovely." When we say something is lovely, we mean it is <u>beautiful,</u> <u>attractive,</u> and <u>delightful</u>. Therefore, she told them that her husband was completely delightful. After all the description, she boldly declared,

> *This is <u>my beloved</u>, and this is <u>my friend</u>,*
>
> *O daughters of Jerusalem.*

She plainly and boldly told them that he was her

"beloved," i.e. he was the person she loved mostly. She tried to tell them, "I love him more than Solomon and every other man." She also called him, "my friend."

You have heard it. Wives, this was a woman like you that perfectly described the worth of her husband. She valued her spouse more that every other person, including Solomon, the wisest man and richest man of his time. This is also a challenge to every husband. Since the Shulamite was able to do this, there is an assignment for everybody. What is the assignment? Perfectly write out all the worth and values of your spouse, in addition to full description of some striking parts of his or her body. Write this as a descriptive essay under a title: "The Invaluable Values of My Spouse."

Make this essay in three copies. Send a copy to me in HAMEO using Godspeople@hameo.org ; a copy to your spouse; and keep the third copy for yourself. When I see your email, I will see how you value your spouse. I hope you'll do better than I expect.

We have been considering the description given by the Shulamite about her spouse. Did her spouse, the beloved, also value her? Yes, he did. Hear the description he gave concerning the Shulamite. He said,

There are threescore queens, and fourscore

concubines, and virgins without number.

My dove, my undefiled is but one; she is

the only one of her mother, she is the choice one of her that bare her. The daughters saw her, and blessed her; yea, the queens and the concubines, and they praised her. (6:8, 9)

He valued her spouse above all queens and concubines. According to him, there were numerous queens and concubines of kings. Solomon had 700 queens and 300 concubines. Yet none can be compared with a little maiden called Shulamite. She had more value than all of them had.

However, this is contrary to what I see and hear nowadays. Many husbands value female ministers, female commissioners, female political leaders, and wives of great leaders than their own wives. What a pity! In the case of the Beloved, the greatest woman before him was his spouse, the Shulamite. He plainly declared in verse nine that the Shulamite was his "one" and "only." He said, "My dove, my undefiled is <u>but ONE;</u> she is the <u>ONLY ONE</u>...the CHOICE ONE." My question to you is "Who is your one and only?"

Now, it is your turn to do the same thing. Song of Solomon is more than a drama; it is a practical guide of how your family should be pattern. Despite the breastless nature, i.e. the low estate and underdeveloped nature of the Shulamite, the Beloved valued and preferred her to all queens and women. In addition, despite the poverty and the nature of the Beloved's job (being a Shepherd) compared to that of Solomon's unlimited riches, the Shulamite valued him and preferred him to all other men in the world.

<u>Your spouse has no any abnormality as you thought or supposed; those features you see as abnormalities are what make him or her unique among others.</u> Value you spouse in every aspect. Prefer him or her to others. Assign great worth to every part of his or her body. Prefer his or her speech to those of others. Fortify yourself with more power of love in order to value your spouse than you have ever done. I wish you best of love for your spouse. Finally, value your spouse as the unique person to marry and live with in this world.

I am the rose of Sharon, and the lily of the valleys. As the lily among thorns, so is my love among the daughters. (2:1, 2)

Part D

INTRODUCTION

For all or almost all manufactured mechanical tools, machines, and some other products, there are some given precautions to be followed in order to prolong the lifespan of such products. So also, it is in marriage. As a fiancé or fiancée, for your marriage with your spouse-to-be not to be supplanted, there are some precautions to adhere to here. Likewise, as a couple, for your marriage not to be interrupted and destroyed, there are some precautions to follow.

In the book of Song of Solomon, there are some inferred precautions for those in courtship and existing couples. Therefore, take this part D very seriously for perpetual enjoyment of your marriage. I wish you best in your home.

Eight

Fight & Reject the Little Foxes of Solomon

What are "the little foxes" of Solomon? Is this term not strange? Yes, it is. Before you can fully understand what I refer to as little foxes of Solomon, I must go back to the main story of the drama.

As I told you earlier, this drama is all about how Solomon brought a young Shulamite woman to his palace as a maiden (an unmarried girl, especially a virgin).

> *Draw me, we will run after thee:* **the king**
>
> **hath brought me into his chambers**:
>
> *we will be glad and rejoice in thee, we will*
>
> *remember thy love more than wine: the*
>
> *upright love thee. (1:4)*

Later, Solomon had desire to marry this maiden. However, Solomon found it difficult to get her in marriage because she was already in courtship with the Beloved. Solomon greatly desired to marry her despite the relationship she had started with the Beloved. As a result, Solomon decided to use everything in his reach to win her love in marriage. To make this effectual, Solomon formed a committee of women that would convince the Shulamite for him. This committee is known as "the daughters of Jerusalem."

Solomon, being the richest, so much used his great wealth, fame, and glory to influence this maiden. Besides, he used the daughters of Jerusalem to convince her day after day. The verses below show the greatness of Solomon and his provision for the daughters of Jerusalem.

Who is this that cometh out of the wilderness like pillars of smoke, perfumed with myrrh and frankincense, with all powders of the merchant? Behold his bed, which is Solomon's; threescore valiant men are about it, of the valiant of Israel. They all hold swords, being expert in war: everyman hath his sword upon his thigh because of fear in the night. King Solomon made himself a chariot of the wood of Lebanon. He made the pillars thereof of silver, the bottom thereof of gold, the covering of it of purple, the midst thereof being paved with love, for the daughters of Jerusalem. Go forth, O ye daughters of Zion, and behold King Solomon with the crown wherewith his mother crowned him

in the day of his espousals, and in the day

of the gladness of his heart. (3:6-11)

The verses are all about the magnificence of Solomon; his formidable security and his possessions and prospects. This is why the last verse (verse 11) was inviting every young woman, including the Shulamite, to see how great Solomon was. This was done to make the Shulamite yield and consent to the proposal of Solomon.

Besides, verse 10 tells us how Solomon provided and furnished good apartments for his committee, the daughters of Jerusalem, in his own magnificent chariot in order to motivate them to fortify their efforts to win the Shulamite for him at all costs. Because of this, the daughters of Jerusalem fought tooth and nail to make the Shulamite marry King Solomon. However, the Shulamite fought back in several occasions and rejected all their offers and suggestions with this rebuke:

I charge you, O ye daughters of

Jerusalem, by the roes, and by the hinds of

the field, that ye stir not up, nor awake

my love, till he please. (2:7; she also said

this in 3:5)

She warned them seriously, "Stir not up, nor awake my love, till he please." That is, do not arouse my love for Solomon until my fiancé will finally be pleased or ready for our wedding. Why did she say that? Their pressure was becoming too much for her. Despite the sharp rebukes she did give to them, they persisted in the business of attempting to win her for Solomon since they were heavily paid for that, in addition to their free accommodation. On the other hand, the Beloved and his friends kept on beckoning to her not to yield to the adversaries' pleas and persuasions. See how they later went to her, pleading that she should not consider the proposal of King Solomon. Hear the interaction of the Shulamite and the Beloved's company in chapter 6:

The Beloved

10 Who is she that looketh forth as the morning, fair as the moon, clear as the sun, and terrible as an army with banners?

The Shulamite

11 I went down into the garden of nuts to see the fruits of the valley, and to see whether the vine flourished, and the pomegranates budded.

12 Or ever I was aware, my soul made me like the chariots of Amminadib.

The Beloved and His Friends

13 <u>Return, return, O Shulamite; return, return, that we may look upon thee</u>. What will ye see in the Shulamite? As it were the company of two armies.

As the Beloved and his friend persuaded her, "Return, return, O Shulamite" unto the Beloved, the daughters of Jerusalem also pleaded with her to return from following the poor Shepherd who would not be able to cater for all her needs. Return from that insecure man who does not have a single bodyguard or security guard like those of King Solomon. "Return, return, O Shulamite" to Solomon the king.

When she and her spouse, the Beloved, discovered that the pressures and the enticements were becoming stronger, they fired a prayer to God for help. What is the prayer? They prayed,

Take us the foxes, the little foxes, that

spoil the vines: for our vines have tender

grapes. (2:15)

They begged God to assist them to prevent and destroy all "little foxes" that were planning to destroy their "vines." What did they mean by vines? The "vines" is a figurative word they used to connote their courtship, wedding, and their marital home.

Then, what are the "foxes" that were planning to destroy their courtship, wedding, and their marital home? These are all the offers, enticements, and persuasions from the daughters of Jerusalem. All these are known as "little foxes of Solomon."

They are little and insignificant but they can make either of the couple to change his or her mind from proceeding into the wedding. They can also cause married couple to be divorced or separated from one another. Beware of little foxes of Solomon.

What do you need to do? You need to fight and reject all little foxes of Solomon that are trying to prevent your wedding or trying to terminate your marriage. You need to frown at and rebuke anyone who comes to you to speak evil of your spouse in order to create hatred in you towards your spouse.

Bachelors and unmarried women, try to be careful lest anybody leads you into wrong marriage. Are you a fiancé or a fiancée? Be informed that many "Solomons" who want to take you from your husband to be or wife to be are in existence. Watch against them and reject all the "little foxes" they will introduce to you. Many of them are very ready to do more than King Solomon did, with the hope that their "little foxes" such as money, promises of luxurious prospects, persuasions and others will entice you.

Some of them are very ready to spend and be spent for "the daughters of Jerusalem" to do the underground work for them. "The daughters of Jerusalem" could be your intimate friends, parents, or other relations. They know that any of these people may easily persuade and change your mind to leave the right person you are to marry in order to marry them. Beware of "the daughters of Jerusalem."

Do not be carried away with any opposite member's wealth, fame, educated status, influence, and prospects. Behave like the Shulamite who was ready to marry the right husband for her, i.e. the poor Beloved, than to marry the richest man, Solomon the king. Always remember that not all that glitters is gold. **The poorest man today can be the richest man tomorrow. Who you are today has no power to limit who you will be**

tomorrow. Tomorrow is not in the hand of who you are today but is in the hand of God who can raise a slave to be the president of a country. Please, and please, do not underrate any man. Therefore, do not mind what "the daughters of Jerusalem" say to win your love for another person.

Ephesians 4:27 says, "Neither give place to the devil." Never laugh with any of the "daughters of Solomon" and never listen to his or her confusing speech and persuasion but give him or her hot frown that will make him or her realize his or her faults. Do not allow your parents and relations to be "the daughters of Jerusalem" against your approved marriage. They may tell you, "You can't marry this poor person." "We don't like that tribe, therefore you cannot marry that your spouse-to-be."

If truly you are led by God, you must obey God, not your parents or any other person. Do you not know that "we ought to obey God rather than men"? (Acts 5:29b). Make sure you are led by God and then do His will by marrying the right person He chooses for you.

Bachelors and unmarried women, be informed that there are innumerable "daughters of Jerusalem" in the world. A man told me how some "daughters of Jerusalem" made attempt to discourage the sister he was led to marry by God. These "daughters of Jerusalem" were in the same church with this brother. They told the sister not to marry him just because the brother was too poor to be married. However, I thank God for the spiritual sister who was also led by God. She did not listen to them but rejected all the "foxes of Solomon" they presented. She married him and God blessed the family mightily with wealth after their wedding. Today, she is highly enjoying her home.

I was in a certain part of the world where there were some "jellyfish" Christians born by some "daughters of Jerusalem." In this area, I was shown a backslider who was once very fervent in the faith and ministry. He was just like an assistant pastor then. What then happened to him? I was told that he was led by God to marry a sister but her parents became "daughters of Jerusalem" against the possibility of the union. They frankly told their daughter not to marry him just because the brother was not a graduate like the sister was. The sister, the jellyfish Christian in the church, obeyed her parents and despised God's leading. The shock was too much for the brother that how this could be done by Christian parents who knew what the will of God was all about in the church.

Who are you jellyfish or doer of God's will? Be informed that you will definitely suffer the consequence of your wrong choice if you take the advice of "the daughters of Jerusalem" who could be your parents, your church members, friends, relations, bosses, neighbours, and so on.

Finally, fight and reject every little fox of Solomon and silence all daughters of Jerusalem in order to do God's will in marriage.

Nine

Never Grieve Your Spouse but Be Prompt to His/Her Request

Another precaution to be taken in marriage or in courtship is to be very careful not to grieve one's spouse or spouse-to-be but to be prompt to his or her request in accordance with God's will. Try as much as possible not to grieve him or her in any matter. Study him or her and know his or her personality and temperament. Accept and take him or her as he or she is and never grieve him or her no matter how he or she seems to be in your sight. For as long as you are sure that he or she is God's will for you to marry, correct him or her and/or talk to God about it.

A problem happened between the Shulamite and the beloved. What happened? Read the Shulamite's report:

> *I sleep, but my heart waketh: it is the voice of my beloved that knocketh, saying, Open to me, my sister, my love, my dove, my undefiled: for my head is filled with dew, and my locks with the drops of the night. I have put off my coat; how shall I put it on? I have washed my feet; how shall I defile them? My beloved put in his hand by the hole of the door, and my bowels were moved for him. I rose up to*

open to my beloved; and my hands dropped with myrrh, and my fingers with sweet smelling myrrh, upon the handles of the lock. I opened to my beloved; but my beloved had withdrawn himself, and was gone: my soul failed when he spake: I sought him, but I could not find him; I called him, but he gave me no answer. The watchmen that went about the city found me, they smote me, they wounded me; the keepers of the walls took away my veil from me. (5:2-7)

I hope you really understand the report. Nevertheless, I know you need more explanation. What happened was that it seemed the Beloved was fond of coming home late in the night. Most times before he got home, it seemed the Shulamite was already asleep. Again, it seemed the Shulamite has corrected him repeatedly. Let's say he obeyed the correction from his spouse.

However, on the fateful day reported in the story above, the Beloved was unable to fulfil the promise due to one thing or the other within or beyond his control. By the time he got home, his spouse was already asleep. This is why she commenced her report with clause, "I sleep."

The Beloved knocked at the door but she refused to open the door because he was too late that night. The Beloved tried and used everything in his reach to beg and apologize but she refused. One, he knocked hard until she woke up from sleep. Two, he pleaded "Open to me," yet she refused. Three, he called her different love-winning names. He called her "<u>my sister, my love, my dove</u>, and <u>my undefiled</u>." Despite these four names, she refused to open the door.

Four, in order to make her sorry for him and then open the door at once, he told her how he was wet with dew and thereby feeling cold. He said, "For my head is filled with dew, and my locks with the drops of the night." Yet, she refused to open the door.

Five, he gave her further reason that he had put off the wet clothes and that he needed to go in to wear dry clothes to reduce the cold and to cover his nakedness. He said, "I have put off my coat; how shall I put it on? I have washed my feet; how shall I defile them?" He made her to know that it was not proper to wear the same wet clothes again. He also told her that he had washed dust and mud from his feet and that he did not want to go back to where he was coming from lest he defiled the feet with dust and mud. However, she failed to listen to him. She has resolved that he should go back to where he was coming from.

Six, in his desperation, he later put his hand or finger in the hole of the door whether he would be able to use his finger to unlock the door himself. He tried and tried, but he was not able. The Shulamite herself testified, *"My beloved put in his hand by the hole of the door"* (Verse 4).

After long time of knocking and waiting, he discovered that all his efforts were to no avail and that it was dangerous for him to sleep outside, he quickly headed another place to sleep. It was after this time, the Shulamite later had compassion on him, but it was too late to cry when the head was already off.

She said, "I opened to my beloved; but my <u>beloved had withdrawn himself, and was gone:</u> my soul failed when he spake: I sought him, but I could not find him; I called him, but he gave me no answer."

It was by this time she regretted what she did. She was very troubled about where he headed alone that silent night. When she could not endure further, she stepped out into the street to look for him. If she had realized earlier that a stitch in time saved nine, she would have made her hay when the sun was shinning. As she went out busy looking for him, the guards saw her and dealt mercilessly with her. She incurred some wounds. She said, "The watchmen...smote me, they wounded me." Besides, her covering cloth was seized.

She said, "The keepers of the walls took away my veil from me."

She suffered many things that night in addition to loneliness and loss of her spouse's company. She suffered all these because she grieved her spouse beyond normal. An adage of ours says, "If a snake is being persistently pursued, it will angrily stop to face and attack the pursuer." This was what happened. When the beloved could not change her mind, he was grieved and withdrew himself.

The same thing was done by Joab in 2 Samuel 2:18-23. Asahel was persistently pursuing Joab to kill him. Joab warned him to return but he did not listen. He was persistent until Joab was grieved and attacked him like a despaired snake and he (Asahel) fell down and died.

Never grieve your spouse or spouse-to-be lest he or she takes wrong steps. Be prompt to his or her requests. If the Shulamite were prompt to the request of her spouse, she would not have suffered all she suffered that night. Avoid anything that can grieve your spouse or spouse-to-be lest he does what will make you to despair your life. Let me illustrate this.

During Samson's wedding, which lasted for seven days, something happened. Samson gave a riddle to thirty Philistines to interpret within the seven days of the wedding. There was a penalty if they fail to interpret the riddle correctly. For them to be free from Samson's penalty, they threatened Samson's bride. She then asked Samson's for the interpretation. After he had told her, she went to reveal the answer to the Philistines. On the seventh day, the thirty men came to Samson and gave him the interpretation of the riddle.

Immediately, Samson was very grieved, stopped to continue the wedding with the bride since she had betrayed him, and revealed the interpretation that Samson gave her to a third party. The story is in Judges 14:10-20. That cancelled the success of the wedding.

Your spouse or spouse-to-be can be grieved in different ways. Study him or her and know his or her dos and don'ts. In the case of Samson, he did not like his secrets to be divulged. He liked confidentiality. **<u>Remember that every spouse wants confidentiality</u>**. Therefore, learn to keep secret lest your spouse or spouse-to-be be grieved. Remember that the failure to do this was the one that made Samson to cancel his wedding with his bride who lacked confidentiality due to threat.

I was told of a man who was beating his wife every time. The more the woman was beaten, the more she endured until a fateful day. What happened on that day? The irresponsible man who had turned himself to a family warrior beat her in the morning on that day. As if that was not enough, in the evening, he started another round of beating. He beat her to the point that she was about to faint or die. It was at this time the woman opened her mouth and said, "Please, don't beat me again. I will die o. Please, don't beat me again so that I will not die."

When the man heard this, he was sorry for her and stopped immediately. This woman was like a dove but she had been maltreated beyond her control. As a result, she left the house without taking any of her clothes or properties. She left but never returned to that house. Why, she was grieved beyond normal.

Please and please, husbands never beat or slap your wives for any reason. Remember that two wrongs never make a right. The Shulamite had a reason why she did not open the door but she later regretted it. **<u>Stop claiming right and do what will not grieve your spouse.</u>**

<u>It is a foolish husband that slaps or beats his wife.</u> Are you a foolish man? Therefore, stop maltreating your wife.

Likewise, whoever you are – wife, husband, fiancé, or fiancée – never grieve your spouse or spouse-to-be with any insult, accusation, and abuse. In addition, **<u>it is a foolish wife or foolish husband</u>**

that abuses and insults his or her spouse. It is a foolish fiancée or foolish fiancé that insults his or her spouse-to-be. Mind how you talk to your spouse or spouse-to-be.

I remember a man that was fond of insulting and abusing his wife. He called her all sorts of bad names. He insulted her publicly before everybody. He had no single respect for her. This continued for very many years. She endured and endured until she could not bear the grievances further. She finally separated from the man, though she continued bearing the man's name.

Never do or say anything that will hurt or grieve your spouse or spouse-to-be. Always remember that human beings can be easily hurt or grieved, among whom your spouse or spouse-to-be is one. Therefore, mind what you do or say to him or her. Learn a lesson from the Shulamite's mistake. No matter the nature of his or her faults, do everything amicably. **Do not allow your marital relationship, which is like an egg, to drop down, and fall apart to the extent that you will not be able to gather it together again.**

Let me sound a resounding and reverberating warning to every fiancé and fiancée. **Courtship is a very delicate entranceway into marriage. Courtship ends at the point of entering into marriage. A terminated or broken courtship is a bar to an anticipated marriage.** This is why many courtships do not give birth to marriage. Since courtship is very delicate and fragile, my warning for you is, be careful not to do or say anything to your spouse-to-be that will make him or her to terminate the courtship, which will consequently debar your marriage.

A young Christian brother was led to marry a young Christian sister. Some of his behaviours and carelessness disgusted the sister. Because of this, out of provocation, she talked to him unadvisedly. She insulted and accused him falsely.

Her speech so much grieved and hurt him that he decided to take a step to stop their anticipated marriage from being conducted. However, before he carried this out, he reported her to his friend in the Lord who told him, "Look before you leap." These words melted the brother's heart and he forgave her.

Therefore, mind what you say or do to whom God gave to you to marry. Despite he or she was given to you by God to marry; he or she can also be discouraged like every other person. **<u>Please, handle your spouse or spouse-to-be with tenderness as if he or she is an egg.</u>**

Another aspect of this precaution I want to draw the attention of everyone to is that you should be prompt to meet the requests of your spouse or spouse-to-be. As a married individual, do not allow your spouse to knock and knock like the Beloved before you open the door for him. Learn a lesson from the Shulamite.

Before I continue, let me sound a warning to everybody in courtship. Be informed that it is not every request of your spouse-to-be you can meet. Any ungodly request must not be met. For instance, if your spouse-to-be asks you to have sex with him or her before your wedding is conducted as a condition to proceed in the courtship with you, do not obey him or her. **<u>It is a useless, irresponsible, and ungodly man or woman that asks for sex before wedding day.</u>** Are you one?

Let him or her know that it is a sinful practice to have sex before wedding (Hebrews 13:4) in amicable way. If he or she persists to have sex first, let the courtship be terminated since he or she is not responsible enough to be married. I pray that God will give you a responsible God-fearing spouse in Jesus' name.

Husbands, be prompt to your wives' requests. Also wives, be prompt to your husbands' requestS. Requests vary from family to family. **Marriage is all about listening than talking. Listen to your spouse always in order to know his or her need at each time. In your priority, let the need of your spouse come first before yours. Instead of enforcing your will always, come to a compromise with your spouse.** For instance, if you like to eat rice and if your spouse is suggesting beans, two of you can come to a compromise by cooking rice and beans together.

Go any length with your spouse as long as his or her request is right in the light of God's word. Here is a lesson: **The more you meet the requests of your spouse, the more you please him or her; and consequently the more he or she will love you. The more your spouse loves you, the more your marriage pillar becomes stronger**. Therefore, **do all things under your reach to build your home (marriage) with hardest bricks of love.**

One of the areas of meeting your spouse's requests is in the area of sex. When he or she requests sex, never deny him or her. The Bible warns, *"Defraud ye not one the other, except it be with consent for a time...Let the husband render unto the wife due benevolence: and likewise also the wife unto the husband."* (1 Corinthians 7:5, 3). Do not be an errant wife or an errant husband. Be faithful.

In addition, if your spouse requests for a secret about yourself, be prompt to tell him or her. Even, without being asked, you should make your entire secrets naked before your spouse. **Nakedness of each husband's or wife's secrets to her or his spouse is one of the major characteristics of marriage. Let your spouse know everything about you. Do not hide anything from him or her but be prompt to reveal all secrets to him or her.** Let me show you example of what the Beloved did when the Shulamite made a request in 1:7, 8.

The Shulamite

Tell me, O thou whom my soul loveth, where thou feedest, where thou makest thy flock to rest at noon: for why should I be

as one that turneth aside by the flocks of
thy companions?

The Beloved

If thou know not, O thou fairest among

women, go thy way forth by the footsteps

of the flock, and feed thy kids beside the

shepherds' tents.

Do you not see the promptness of the Beloved's answer to the Shulamite's request? The Shulamite asked, "Where" is this and that? In response, the Beloved revealed everything to her without hiding anything from her. He said, "Go thy way" to so and so.

This is what is expected of you. Tell your spouse all about you. Let your spouse know your investments and accounts. For as long as your spouse is your best half, nothing that you – one-half of the body (couple) – know that he or she should not know. Be plain to her.

Personally, what I desire most in marriage is plainness and openness. Therefore, for me to be highly pleased with my wife, she must be totally opened

and plain to me. Do not hide anything from your spouse. This is what increases marital joy. What is the precaution here again? Never grieve or hurt your spouse but be prompt to meet his or her requests in accordance with God's will. Therefore, if your spouse suggests abortion in order to terminate unplanned or unwanted pregnancy, you must not grant that devilish request. Be wise!

Moreover, **you must not grant any request that will make you connive with your spouse to do evil.** The Scripture says, "Thou **shalt not follow** a multitude to do evil..." (Exodus 23:3) "My son, if sinners entice thee, **consent thou not**" (Proverbs 1:10). "If thy brother...or the WIFE of thy bosom...entice thee secretly, saying, Let us go and serve other gods...**thou shalt not consent unto him**, nor hearken unto him; neither shall thine eye pity him..." (Deuteronomy 13:6, 8)

Let us assume that your spouse calls and tells you, "Darling, if truly you love me, you must hate what I hate, and love what I love. Do you know Mr So-and-so? He offended me seriously. In addition, I have resolved not to interact with him again. Therefore, if you see him or his family members, do not greet them. And if anyone of them greets you, don't respond." My friend, you must not consent to that request. The Bible says that we should not keep malice but we should live together in love and peace.

Likewise, your spouse may say, "Honey, I'm very tired now; I want to go and have my siesta. If anybody comes to ask of me, tell him or her that I'm not at home." You must not consent to speak lies before God.

Summarily, listen to and study your spouse or spouse-to-be always and never grieve or hurt him or her just for any reason but be prompt to grant his or her requests in accordance with God's word. Couples, I wish you more joy in your home. Likewise, I wish all lawful and right couples-to-be unbroken courtships that will lead to successful weddings coupled with happy homes of unlimited joy and love in Jesus' name.

Ten

Never Be Ashamed of Your Spouse but Be Proud of Him or Her

The third marital precaution inferred from the drama is for one not to be ashamed of one's spouse but to be highly proud of him or her anywhere, anytime. Many a wife is ashamed of her husband and vice versa. They prefer going alone than to be in company of their spouses.

I like something greatly in this drama. The Beloved and the Shulamite were so proud of each other. They were never ashamed of each other. Despite the nature of the Beloved's job, being an ordinary shepherd, and the personality of the Shulamite, they were never ashamed of each other in anywhere and before anybody.

The Shulamite was very proud of him before her parent (mother). She was ready to talk about him before her mother and to take him to her mother. Hear what she said:

> *O that thou wert as my brother, that sucked the breasts of my mother! when I should find thee without, I would kiss thee; yea, I should not be despised. I would lead thee, and bring thee into my mother's house, who would instruct me: I*

would cause thee to drink of spiced wine

of the juice of my pomegranate. (8:1,2)

As an unmarried woman, she was bold to bring the Beloved to her mother and tell her, "Mummy, this is the man I want to marry." Despite all criticisms, oppositions, and problems they face, she was never ashamed to be identified with him before her parent. She even affirmed, "Yea, I should not be despised." See what she did again:

It was but a little that I passed from them,

but I found him whom my soul loveth: I

held him, and would not let him go, until

I had brought him into my mother's

house, and into he chamber of her that

conceived me.(3:4)

Again, the Shulamite was never ashamed of the Beloved before strangers and anybody in the city and in the country. She was proud of him more than anybody and anything else. See what she did:

The watchmen that go about the city

found me: to whom I said, Saw ye him

whom my soul loveth?(3:3)

She boldly talked about her husband before security guards who were strangers to her. Everywhere and every time, she was very ready to die than to deny or to be ashamed of her husband. How about you, are you ready to do likewise? This is a lesson for you to learn. Let all people know that he or she is your spouse.

Another thing we see is that both of them were not ashamed to identify with each other before their friends. Can you show your friends, "This is my own husband," "This is my own wife," "This is my fiancé (fiancée)"? Be proud of him or her everywhere. Listen to how the Beloved was bidding his friends to celebrate with him and his wife:

I am come into my garden, my sister, my

spouse: I have gathered my myrrh with

my spice; I have eaten my honey comb

with my honey; I have drunk my wine

with my milk: eat, O FRIENDS; drink,

yea, drink abundantly, O beloved.(5:1)

The Shulamite did a thing that challenges me greatly. What is it? She was highly proud of her spouse before all her antagonists who despised her marital relationship. Who are these opposers? These are the daughters of Jerusalem." She told them,

> *I charge you, O daughters of Jerusalem, if*
>
> *ye find my beloved, that ye tell him, that I*
>
> *am sick of love. (5:8)*

When "the daughters of Jerusalem" heard this speech of unquenchable love, their heads and hearts sparked vehemently. They asked her to tell them the useless spouse that was causing her to be sick of love. They asked reproachfully, "…What is thy beloved more than another beloved, that thou dost so charge us?" (5:9).

She took pain to describe her spouse beautifully from A to Z without any iota of shame. What a lesson for you to learn! She started the description from verse ten and ended it in verse sixteen. She boldly declared with full pride about her spouse,

> <u>*This is my beloved,*</u> *and this is my friend,*
>
> *O daughters of Jerusalem. (5:16b)*

Can you not perceive her confidence? She said, "This is my beloved." She was not afraid of her opposers and despisers. She did not allow their intimidation and evil speaking to make her deny her husband. Do you know that many husbands and many wives are ashamed to identify with their spouses in the presence of those that despise, blaspheme, and mock their spouses?

This reminds me what happened a day when one of my children in the Lord and I were standing together and talking by the roadside. Suddenly, she told me, "I want to quickly go inside my house so that brother A (name withheld) will not meet me here." She added that he would be coming to see one of her neighbours. I rebuked her immediately, "Are you ashamed of me? Stand here and let him meet you here! Why do you fear brother A criticism than be proud of me as your spiritual father?"

Two years later, I went to visit the same town and visited the same sister who is my daughter in the Lord. As I was talking, I called her, "My sister." She interrupted me and corrected me, "Don't call me your sister." This baffled me and I asked, "Why did you say so?" She then declared to me, "I am your daughter, not your sister. This is because brother and sister can quarrel and be separated from each other forever but a father and his child ever remain cordial."

This person was once ashamed of me. Now she is proud of having me as her father in the Lord. Even before I went to visit her, she had proudly discussed me before her neighbours that had not seen me before that she had a wonderful father in the Lord.

Emulate this sister. She was once ashamed of me but later became very proud of me. Have you been ashamed of your spouse until now before those that despise, criticize, and mock him or her? Now, go back to them and be proud of him or her before them all. Tell them like the Shulamite, "This is my beloved." Tell them, "This is my one and only." Let me show you some of the confessions of the Shulamite to everybody around her. She boldly declared,

> *My beloved is mine, and I am his: he feedeth among the lilies. (2:16)*

> *I am my beloved's, and my beloved is mine: he feedeth among the lilies. (6:3)*

> *I am my beloved's, and his desire is toward me. (7:10)*

You, too, boldly declare to others, "My beloved is mine, and I am his." Never be ashamed of his or her appearance, status, outlook, physique, predicament, financial status, and so on. Tell everybody that needs to know, "I am my beloved's and my beloved is mine."

Besides telling them with your mouth, act it out before them to see. Remember that action speaks louder than voice. Act it out by being associating with your spouse always. **The more people see you and your spouse together every time in everywhere, the more they easily conclude and say, "See how this couple love and are proud of each other."**

There was a great association between the Shulamite. In 7:10, the Shulamite reports, "… his desire is toward me." Can you now see how the husband always desired to stay and associate with his wife? Did the wife let him down? No! The wife told him to come so that both of them will walk together without any shame. In the next verse, 7:11, she invites,

> *Come, my beloved, let us go forth into the field; let us lodge in the villages.*

She did not say, "Go on your own, and I'll go on my own. We'll meet over there." She insisted that they would go together. She said, "Come…let us go…"

This is a great lesson for you. Associate with your spouse everywhere. **Anywhere that I will be ashamed to go with my wife is not worth**

going for me. I am a half while my wife is the other half. Until my wife and I come together before we become one. What about you and your spouse, are you one or two? My wife and I are an inseparable body or entity. We are never two but one. This is why we cannot do without each other.

Anything that is good for you is good for your spouse. Therefore, never be ashamed to associate with your spouse anywhere. Be proud of him or her before anybody – your parents, relations, friends, neighbours, co-workers, church members, and any other man – without any iota of shame. I like a couple greatly in the Bible. This is Aquila and Priscilla (Acts 18:2,3; 19:26). They both associated in everything and in everywhere. They worked and walked together. When the Bible is talking about Aquila, it must also talk about Priscilla. What a great couple!

This is a beautiful pattern for your family. **The more you become associating with your spouse, the more you are proud of him or her, the more your home (family) becomes stronger against circumstances that terminate marriages.**

Eleven

Involve God in Your Courtship & Marriage Relationship

Any home where Christ is left out is a home of crisis. It is observed that many couples and many couples-to-be who want good homes often leave Christ out in their planning. **A home where Christ is missing often faces confusion, troubles, problems, stagnancy, and backwardness.**

Let me illustrate this from the Scripture. When Jesus Christ was missing from the company of his parents on their way back from the feast in Jerusalem, what happened? Immediately, confusion, sorrow, and troubles of mind visited the parents. This then stopped their progress and brought backwardness upon them. See the story in Luke 2:41-48.

Your courtship may not go far without Christ. Your home cannot get to the perfect sweetness if Christ is not in it. Bear in mind that many forces militate against marriage and courtship.

Several spiritual forces fight against courtship and marriage. Satan and his agents fight day and night to destroy the original good plans of God for homes.

Several human forces also fight against the success of courtship and marriage. Relatives-in-law that do not agree with the marriage fight directly or indirectly to put a stop to the courtship or the marriage. They may refuse to give their consents for the wedding to proceed. The disappointed people who desired or desire to marry you or marry your spouse also wage war to ensure the failure of your wedding or the dissolution of your marriage. Envious couples whose homes are not settled also desire that your home should be unsettled like theirs. Likewise, envious relatives, especially those whose children you are better than, wish the failure and the evil of your marriage.

These two groups of forces – evil spiritual beings and unsatisfied human beings – often cause much havocs to courtship and marriage. They cause the premature death, insanity, discouragement to one of the couple-to-be, and so on. These forces also sour many marriages with barrenness, infertility, sicknesses, poverty, mysterious occurrences, children's death, spiritual attacks, death of a spouse, and so on.

Many other forces against marriage and courtship exist. However, let me limit my discussion to the few ones I have referred to here.

Many factors are also needed for the success of courtship and marriage. Such factors include wisdom and skills to management the home and the relationship. They also include money to conduct the wedding and to finance the family after wedding. Other factors include grace for children's training, patience to bear and dwell with your spouse as a couple, and so on.

With the existence of all these forces and factors, your courtship and/or your marriage may not go far if you fail to involve Christ into your courtship and marriage.

The Beloved and the Shulamite faced different factors and forces, which would have hampered the success of their marriage if they had not involved God. They prayed to God to help them deal with all the forces that militated against their courtship and marriage. Solomon, the covetous human force, wanted the Shulamite as a wife at all costs. He employed all manners of "foxes" to devour the success of the marriage of the Shulamite with the Beloved. However, they involved God and fired prayer to God for help against all the activities of Solomon against their marriage. They prayed thus:

> *Take us the foxes, the little foxes, that*
>
> *spoil the vines: for our vines have tender*
>
> *grapes. (2:15)*

They cried to God to help them take away all the forces against their marriage. God answered them and they had a happy home.

For you to have a happy home, you must emulate

the Beloved's family. You must involve God into your courtship and marriage. How do you involve God into your family?

One, you must establish a sound relationship between you and God first. To do this, you and your spouse must submit yourselves to God and be born again. You must repent and turn away from all your sins; and then accept Jesus as your Lord and as the Head of your family.

Two, your family must be a praying type. You must give yourselves to prayer. Remember that all the forces against courtship and marriage are very many that you cannot but afford to involve a Higher Being (God) from Heaven to help you fight them and give you the desired success. The Beloved and his spouse knew this fact and they prayed.

Begin your courtship and family with prayer; run the family with prayer. Fast healthily as much as possible. Let God be the number one Person in your family. Again, bear in mind that if you are not born again, your prayers are in vain. God does not answer the prayers of sinners with the exception of few cases of mercy. *"Now we know that God heareth not sinners: but if any man be a worshipper of God, and doeth his will, him he heareth"* (John 9:31). *"If I regard iniquity in my heart, the*

Lord will not hear me" (Psalms 66:18)

Do you have a collapsing home – wayward children or immoral spouse? You can single-handedly repair this home if you can submit yourself to God first and then fight the situation with serious prayers. This is a message for parents, especially those with wayward children, who want God to transform their children. You yourself need to be transformed first.

Now, let me tell you little about our courtship. My wife and I began our courtship with fasting and prayer and ran the whole courtship with regular fasting and prayer. The table below is the timetable of our courtship activity, which spanned six months.

LM COURTSHIP AND WEDDING TIMETABLE

PERIOD	WEEK/ MEETING	DATE	ACTIVITY/ DISCUSSION
	1	31-Jan	FASTING & PRAYER
COURTSHIP PERIOD	2	7-Feb	**TOPIC 1a: BIOGRAPHY OF HUSBAND TO BE**
		8-Feb	
	3	14-Feb	**TOPIC 1b: BIOGRAPHY OF WIFE TO BE**
	4	21-Feb	FASTING & PRAYER
		22-Feb	
	5	28-Feb	**TOPIC 2: MY IDEAL WIFE**

6	7-Mar	**TOPIC 3: MY IDEAL HUSBAND**
	8-Mar	
7	14-Mar	FASTING & PRAYER
8	21-Mar	SERMON 1:
	22-Mar	
9	28-Mar	**TOPIC 4: MONEY MANAGEMENT IN THE HOME**
10	4-Apr	FASTING & PRAYER
11	11-Apr	SERMON 2:
	12-Apr	
12	18-Apr	**TOPIC 5: OUR PLANS FOR OUR EXTENDED FAMILY**
	19-Apr	
13	25-Apr	FASTING & PRAYER
14	2-May	BOOK DISCUSSION 1:
15	9-May	**TOPIC 6: PRACTICAL MARRIAGE PLANS**
	10-May	
16	16-May	FASTING & PRAYER/SERMON 3
17	23-May	**TOPIC 7: COMBINING WORK WITH HOME**
	24-May	
18	30-May	FASTING & PRAYER
19	6-Jun	SERMON 4:
20	13-Jun	**TOPIC 8: WORKING FOR GOD & CARING FOR HOME**
	14-Jun	
21	20-Jun	**TOPIC 9: CAREER AND MARRIAGE**
22	27-Jun	FASTING & PRAYER

		28-Jun	
	23	4-Jul	BOOK DISCUSSION 2:
	24	11-Jul	WEDDING PLANNING
POST-COURTSHIP PERIOD		12-Jul	
	25	18-Jul	**PROPOSED BRIDE PRICE PAYMENT DAY (TRADITIONAL WEDDING)**
	26	25-Jul	
		26-Jul	
	27	1-Aug	
	28	8-Aug	**PROPOSED WEDDING DAY (WHITE WEDDING)**
	29	15-Aug	
	30	22-Aug	
	31	29-Aug	
	32	5-Sep	
	33	12-Sep	

You can see from the timetable that we started with fasting and prayer. Within the six-month courtship period, we had meetings for 24 times. Within these 24 meetings, we spent eight meetings on fasting and prayer. We spent one-third of our courtship meetings on fasting and prayer. With this, God really helped us.

2, 8%

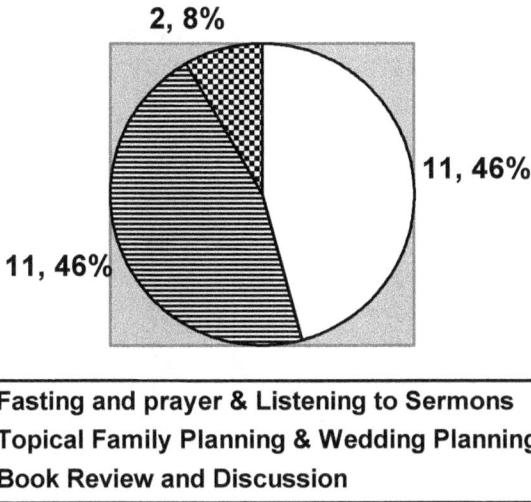

11, 46%

11, 46%

□ Fasting and prayer & Listening to Sermons
🬋 Topical Family Planning & Wedding Planning
⊠ Book Review and Discussion

In addition to that, we also engaged ourselves in finishing the whole Bible within the six-month period of our courtship. Despite my heavy busy schedule of work in the bank, in my workplace then, I was able to do this effectively. Likewise did my fiancée then who is now my wife. The tables below are the reading plan we used. You can use that also for yours if you care.

DAYS	DATE	BIBLE PASSAGE	NO OF CHAPTERS PER DAY	CHAPTERS READ SO FAR
		JANUARY (Month 1)		
1	1-Jan	GEN 1-7	7	7
2	2-Jan	GEN 8-14	7	14
3	3-Jan	GEN 15-21	7	21
4	4-Jan	GEN 22-28	7	28
5	5-Jan	GEN 29-35	7	35
6	6-Jan	GEN 36-42	7	42
7	7-Jan	GEN 43-49	7	49
8	8-Jan	GEN 50-EXO 6	7	56
9	9-Jan	EXO 7-13	7	63
10	10-Jan	EXO 14-20	7	70
11	11-Jan	EXO 21-27	7	77
12	12-Jan	EXO 28-34	7	84
13	13-Jan	EXO 35-LEV 1	7	91
14	14-Jan	LEV 2-8	7	98
15	15-Jan	LEV 9-15	7	105
16	16-Jan	LEV 16-22	7	112
17	17-Jan	LEV 23-NUM 2	7	119
18	18-Jan	NUM 3-9	7	126
19	19-Jan	NUM 10-16	7	133
20	20-Jan	NUM 17-23	7	140
21	21-Jan	NUM 24-30	7	147
22	22-Jan	NUM 31-DEU 1	7	154
23	23-Jan	DEU 2-8	7	161
24	24-Jan	DEU 9-15	7	168
25	25-Jan	DEU 16-22	7	175
26	26-Jan	DEU 23-29	7	182
27	27-Jan	DEU 30-JOS 2	7	189
28	28-Jan	JOS 3-9	7	196
29	29-Jan	JOS 10-16	7	203
30	30-Jan	JOS 17-23	7	210
31	31-Jan	JOS 24- JDG 6	7	217

DAYS	DATE	BIBLE PASSAGE	NO OF CHAPTERS PER DAY	NO OF CHAPTERS READ SO FAR
		FEBRUARY (Month 2)		
32	1-Feb	JDG 7-13	7	224
33	2-Feb	JDG 14-20	7	231
34	3-Feb	JDG 21- I SAM 2	7	238
35	4-Feb	I SAM 3-9	7	245
36	5-Feb	I SAM 10-16	7	252
37	6-Feb	I SAM 17-23	7	259
38	7-Feb	I SAM 24-30	7	266
39	8-Feb	I SAM 31- II SAM 6	7	273
40	9-Feb	I I SAM 7-13	7	280
41	10-Feb	I I SAM 14-20	7	287
42	11-Feb	I I SAM 21- I KGS 3	7	294
43	12-Feb	I KGS 4-10	7	301
44	13-Feb	I KGS 11-17	7	308
45	14-Feb	I KGS 18-II KGS 2	7	315
46	15-Feb	II KGS 3-9	7	322
47	16-Feb	II KGS 10-16	7	329
48	17-Feb	II KGS 17-23	7	336
49	18-Feb	II KGS 24- I CHR 5	7	343
50	19-Feb	I CHR 6-12	7	350
51	20-Feb	I CHR 13-19	7	357
52	21-Feb	I CHR 20-26	7	364
53	22-Feb	I CHR 27-II CHR 4	7	371
54	23-Feb	II CHR 5-11	7	378
55	24-Feb	II CHR 12-18	7	385
56	25-Feb	II CHR 19-25	7	392
57	26-Feb	II CHR 26-32	7	399
58	27-Feb	II CHR 33- EZR 3	7	406
59	28-Feb	EZR 4-10	7	413

DAYS	DATE	BIBLE PASSAGE	NO OF CHAPTERS PER DAY	NO OF CHAPTERS READ SO FAR
		MARCH (Month 3)		
60	1-Mar	NEH 1-7	7	420
61	2-Mar	NEH 8- ESTH 1	7	427
62	3-Mar	ESTH 2-8	7	434
63	4-Mar	ESTH 9- JOB 5	7	441
64	5-Mar	JOB 6-12	7	448
65	6-Mar	JOB 13-19	7	455
66	7-Mar	JOB 20-26	7	462
67	8-Mar	JOB 27-33	7	469
68	9-Mar	JOB 34-40	7	476
69	10-Mar	JOB 41-PS 5	7	483
70	11-Mar	PS 6-12	7	490
71	12-Mar	PS 13-19	7	497
72	13-Mar	PS 20-26	7	504
73	14-Mar	PS 27-33	7	511
74	15-Mar	PS 34-40	7	518
75	16-Mar	PS 41-47	7	525
76	17-Mar	PS 48-54	7	532
77	18-Mar	PS 55-61	7	539
78	19-Mar	PS 62-68	7	546
79	20-Mar	PS 69-75	7	553
80	21-Mar	PS 76-82	7	560
81	22-Mar	PS 83-89	7	567
82	23-Mar	PS 90-96	7	574
83	24-Mar	PS 97-103	7	581
84	25-Mar	PS 104-110	7	588
85	26-Mar	PS 111-117	7	595
86	27-Mar	PS 118-119	2	597
87	28-Mar	PS 120-126	7	604
88	29-Mar	PS 127-133	7	611
89	30-Mar	PS 134-140	7	618
90	31-Mar	PS 141-147	7	625

DAYS	DATE	BIBLE PASSAGE	NO OF CHAPTERS PER DAY	NO OF CHAPTERS READ SO FAR
		APRIL (Month 4)		
91	1-Apr	PS 148- PROV 4	7	632
92	2-Apr	PROV 5-11	7	639
93	3-Apr	PROV 12-18	7	646
94	4-Apr	PROV 19-25	7	653
95	5-Apr	PROV 26-ECCL 1	7	660
96	6-Apr	ECCL 2-8	7	667
97	7-Apr	ECCL 9- SSOL 3	7	674
98	8-Apr	SSOL 4- ISA 2	7	681
99	9-Apr	ISA 3-9	7	688
100	10-Apr	ISA 10-16	7	695
101	11-Apr	ISA 17-23	7	702
102	12-Apr	ISA 24-30	7	709
103	13-Apr	ISA 31-37	7	716
104	14-Apr	ISA 38-44	7	723
105	15-Apr	ISA 45-51	7	730
106	16-Apr	ISA 52-58	7	737
107	17-Apr	ISA 59-65	7	744
108	18-Apr	ISA 66- JER 6	7	751
109	19-Apr	JER 7-13	7	758
110	20-Apr	JER 14-20	7	765
111	21-Apr	JER 21-27	7	772
112	22-Apr	JER 28-34	7	779
113	23-Apr	JER 35-41	7	786
114	24-Apr	JER 42-48	7	793
115	25-Apr	JER 49- LAM 3	7	800
116	26-Apr	LAM 4- EZEK 5	7	807
117	27-Apr	EZEK 6-12	7	814
118	28-Apr	EZEK 13-19	7	821
119	29-Apr	EZEK 20-26	7	828
120	30-Apr	EZEK 27-33	7	835

DAYS	DATE	BIBLE PASSAGE	CHAPTERS PER DAY	CHAPTERS READ SO FAR
		MAY (Month 5)		
121	1-May	EZEK 34-40	7	842
122	2-May	EZEK 41-47	7	849
123	3-May	EZEK 48 - DAN 6	7	856
124	4-May	DAN 7- HOS 1	7	863
125	5-May	HOS 2-8	7	870
126	6-May	HOS 9- JOEL 1	7	877
127	7-May	JOEL 2- AMOS 5	7	884
128	8-May	AMOS 6- JONAH 2	7	891
129	9-May	JONAH 3- MIC 5	7	898
130	10-May	MIC 6- HAB 2	7	905
131	11-May	HAB 3- ZECH 1	7	912
132	12-May	ZECH 2-8	7	919
133	13-May	ZECH 9- MAL 1	7	926
134	14-May	MAL 2- MATT 4	7	933
135	15-May	MATT 5-11	7	940
136	16-May	MATT 12-18	7	947
137	17-May	MATT 19-25	7	954
138	18-May	MATT 26- MARK 4	7	961
139	19-May	MARK 5-11	7	968
140	20-May	MARK 12- LUKE 2	7	975
141	21-May	LUKE 3-9	7	982
142	22-May	LUKE 10-16	7	989
143	23-May	LUKE 17-23	7	996
144	24-May	LUKE 24- JOHN 6	7	1003
145	25-May	JOHN 7- 13	7	1010
146	26-May	JOHN 14-20	7	1017
147	27-May	JOHN 21- ACTS 6	7	1024
148	28-May	ACTS 7-13	7	1031
149	29-May	ACTS 14-20	7	1038
150	30-May	ACTS 21-27	7	1045
151	31-May	ACTS 28- ROM 6	7	1052

DAYS	DATE	BIBLE PASSAGE	NO OF CHAPTERS PER DAY	NO OF CHAPTERS READ SO FAR
		JUNE (Month 6)		
152	1-Jun	ROM 7-13	7	1059
153	2-Jun	ROM 14- I COR 4	7	1066
154	3-Jun	I COR 5-11	7	1073
155	4-Jun	I COR 12- IICOR 2	7	1080
156	5-Jun	II COR 3-9	7	1087
157	6-Jun	II COR 10- GAL 3	7	1094
158	7-Jun	GAL 4- EPH 4	7	1101
159	8-Jun	EPH 5- COL 1	7	1108
160	9-Jun	COL 2- I THES 4	7	1115
161	10-Jun	I THES 5- I TIM 3	7	1122
162	11-Jun	I TIM 4 - II TIM 4	7	1129
163	12-Jun	TIT 1- HEB 3	7	1136
164	13-Jun	HEB 4-10	7	1143
165	14-Jun	HEB 11- JAM 4	7	1150
166	15-Jun	JAM 5- II PET 1	7	1157
167	16-Jun	II PET 2- I JOHN 5	7	1164
168	17-Jun	II JOHN - REV 4	7	1171
169	18-Jun	REV 5-11	7	1178
170	19-Jun	REV 12-18	7	1185
171	20-Jun	REV 19-22	4	1189
172	21-Jun		****	
173	22-Jun	TOTAL CHAPTERS=	1189	
174	23-Jun			
175	24-Jun			
176	25-Jun			
177	26-Jun			
178	27-Jun			
179	28-Jun			
180	29-Jun			
181	30-Jun			

Today, I am very happy with my home. God is the Ruler, the Head, and the Defender of our family. Today, we regularly observe daily period of family prayers every afternoon besides the normal family devotion in the morning. The family that prays and serves God together stays together. You too need to involve God into your own family. Bring Jesus into your relationship and courtship today.

Part E

THE WINNING ACTS OF LOVE

INTRODUCTION

Proverbs 18:19 says, "A brother offended is harder to be WON than a strong city..." Generally, human beings are difficult to be won. As a married person, for a happy marriage to remain to the end, you must win the love of your spouse. To do this, you have some obligations to carry out. These are the winning acts of love. They are well explained in all the chapters of this Part E. Let us consider them one by one.

Twelve

Praise & Quality Your Spouse Always

One of the commonest things I see in the book of Song of Solomon is the praise that the couple gave to each other. **Praising of one's spouse makes him or her to love one more dearly and this consequently strengthens the foundation and pillars of one's marriage.** This is another secret or tip for a successful marriage. **Praising and qualifying one's spouse always is a great tool in marriage for winning his or her love.** The beloved knew this well and made this a serious business to engage himself throughout the play. He started this from the outset of the play, from chapter one. In Chapter one, he said,

> *If thou know not, <u>O thou fairest among women</u>, go thy way forth by the footsteps of the flock, and feed thy kids beside the shepherds' tents. I have compared thee, O my love, to a company of horses in Pharaoh's chariots. Thy cheeks are comely with rows of jewels, thy neck with chains of gold. (1:8-10)*

When the Shulamite, his wife, heard this, she saw herself to be somebody before her husband. This made her to feel at home and shower great praises on her husband who loved her dearly. She voiced out,

> *While the king sitteth at his table, my spikenard sendeth forth the smell thereof. A bundle of myrrh is my well beloved unto me; he shall lie all night betwixt my breasts. My beloved is unto me as a cluster of camphire in the vineyards of Engedi. <u>Behold, thou art fair, my beloved, yea, pleasant</u>: also our bed is green. The beams of our house are cedar, and our rafters of fir. (1:12-14, 16, 17)*

Do you not see how the husband and his wife praised and qualified each other? This made each one of them to see himself or herself as a loved and desired person before his or her spouse. The praises generated untold love in them. The love was so strong that none of "the foxes" of Solomon could devour it. Their regular praises fortified their love for each other, which thereby fortified the marriage against Solomon's efforts to separate them.

There is power in praise. Delight to praise your spouse than looking for faults to blame on him or her. Praise your spouse always. Look at it. In chapter one of Song of Solomon, they praised each other. They did not stop there. Later in chapter two, the Beloved gave additional praise by saying, "For sweet is thy voice, and thy countenance is comely" (2:14b). **<u>Never be tired in praising your spouse. Praise your spouse to his or her hearing.</u>** Some people are fond of praising their spouses in their absence before others. Why do they do this? They say and think that if he or she hears it, he or she may relax and do below expectation. No, it is not so!

Let him or her hear the praise with his or her ears. This will make him or her to see that he or she is highly appreciated and loved by you. Most praises found in Song of Solomon were said directly to the praised persons, not in their absence. This explains the reason for the indissolubility of their marriage by all negative circumstances and "foxes" that attacked it. **While praising your spouse, let the characteristics of the praises be the qualities that he or she possesses. Qualify everything you can see in him or her. Qualify every part of his or her <u>body</u>. Qualify his or her <u>goodness and virtues.</u>**

Qualify his or her <u>beauty</u>. Qualify his or her <u>speech.</u> Qualify his or her <u>manner of doing things.</u> Qualify his or her <u>greatness and achievement in life.</u> Qualify <u>every good thing</u> you perceive in his or her life.
This is what the Beloved spent chapter four of the play on. Hear how he did it.

Behold, thou art fair, my love; behold, thou art fair; thou hast doves' eyes within thy locks: thy hair is as a flock of goats, that appear from mount Gilead. Thy teeth are like a flock of sheep that are even shorn, which came up from the washing; whereof every one bear twins, and none is barren among them. Thy lips are like a thread of scarlet, and thy speech is comely: thy temples are like a piece of a pomegranate within thy locks. Thy neck is like the tower of David builded for an armoury, whereon there hang a thousand bucklers, all shields of mighty men. Thy two breasts are like two young roes that are twins, which feed among the lilies. Until the day break, and the shadows flee away, I will get me to the mountain of myrrh, and to the hill of frankincense. Thou art all fair, my love; there is no spot in thee. Come with me from Lebanon, my spouse, with me from Lebanon: look from the top of Amana, from the top of Shenir and Hermon, from the lions' dens, from the mountains of the leopards. Thou hast ravished my heart, my sister, my spouse; thou hast ravished my heart with one of thine eyes, with one chain of thy neck. How fair is thy love, my sister, my spouse! how much better is thy love than wine! and the smell of thine ointments than all spices! Thy lips, O my spouse, drop as the honeycomb: honey and milk are under thy tongue; and the smell of thy garments is like the smell of Lebanon. A garden inclosed is my sister, my spouse; a spring shut up, a fountain sealed. Thy plants are an orchard of pomegranates, with pleasant fruits; camphire, with spikenard, Spikenard and saffron; calamus and cinnamon, with all trees of frankincense; myrrh and aloes, with all the chief spices: A fountain of gardens, a

well of living waters, and streams from Lebanon.
(4:1-15)

Now, you have learnt it from the Beloved. From now onward, **do not allow a day to pass away without dropping at least a small fragment of praise on your spouse.** Shower your spouse with praise always. He or she demands it than you think. **As God cherishes praises greatly, so also your spouse, His creature, likes to be praised by you.**

Now let us be practical. **When you wake up in the morning, before you leave for work, praise your spouse. When you return from work, praise him or her. Moreover, before you sleep in the night, soak him or her in the river of praises from your mouth.** Will you do this?

This is what we see in the Beloved, right from chapter one, he had been praising his wife. He did not stop there; he continued in chapter two. When he got to chapter four, the praises became ocean as seen above. After this, he did not assume that the ocean of praise was sufficient for his wife, but he added refreshing dews of praise in chapter six. What are we learning from these? **No amount of praise can be too much for your spouse.** In chapter six, he praised her thus,

Thou art beautiful, O my love, as Tirzah, comely as Jerusalem, terrible as an army with banners. Turn away thine eyes from me, for they have overcome me: thy hair is as a flock of goats that appear from Gilead. Thy teeth are as a flock of sheep which go up from the washing, whereof every one beareth twins, and there is not one barren among them. As a piece of a pomegranate are thy temples within thy locks. There are threescore queens, and fourscore concubines, and virgins without number. My dove, my undefiled is but one; she is the only one of her mother, she is the choice one of her that bare her. The daughters saw her, and blessed her; yea, the queens and the concubines, and they praised her. Who is she that looketh forth as the morning, fair as the moon, clear as the sun, and terrible as an army with banners? (6:4-10)

When last did you tell your spouse, "Thou (you) are beautiful"? He or she wants to hear this. Tell him or her. One of the commonest clauses I see in this book of Song of Solomon is "Thou art fair" or "Thou art all fair." You can vividly see this in many verses quoted in this chapter eleven of this book. If the whole world combines to tell your spouse, "You are too ugly," that may not bother him or her for as long as he or she keeps on hearing you saying to him or her, "You are the most beautiful (or handsome) person I have ever seen; even you are the most beautiful queen (or handsome king) and angel to me."

However, if you are the one that tells him or her, "I don't even know how God created you. You are too ugly, even uglier than the ugliest element in the world," he or she will see himself or herself inferior in the society. I have told you earlier that your spouse is the unique person in this life to you. Always tell him or her, "Darling, you are very fair and beautiful (or handsome) indeed. I am very lucky to have you as my spouse."

To describe further how beautiful she was, the Beloved said in that chapter six above, "Turn away thine eyes from me, for they have overcome me." He was trying to tell her that she was so beautiful to look at without one being prompted to marry her. Qualify your spouse greatly than he or she thinks he or she is. From henceforth, **do not be a faultfinder but a praise-giver to your spouse.**

Praise your spouse for whatever good he or she did. **Always appreciate the food cooked by your wife. Each time, she serves you food, commend her for the sweetness of the meal. In addition, whenever your spouse gives you money or buys something for you, praise him or her for it, no matter how small or few it may be.** Be a praise-giver always. Until you die, never stop to praise your spouse. The Beloved did not stop after the dews of praise in chapter six; he went further and poured a mighty rain of praise in chapter seven. Here is the rain of praise that he sent to water and to qualify every part of her body and physique:

How beautiful are thy feet with shoes, O prince's daughter! the joints of thy thighs are like jewels, the work of the hands of a cunning workman. Thy navel is like a round goblet, which wanteth not liquor: thy belly is like an heap of wheat set about with lilies. Thy two breasts are like two young roes that are twins. Thy neck is as a tower of ivory; thine eyes like the fish pools in Heshbon, by the gate of Bathrabbim: thy nose is as the tower of Lebanon which looketh toward Damascus. Thine head upon thee is like Carmel, and the hair of thine head like purple; the king is held in the galleries. How fair and how pleasant art thou, O love, for delights! This thy stature is like to a palm tree, and thy breasts to clusters of grapes. I said, I will go up to the palm tree, I will take hold of the boughs thereof: now also thy breasts shall be as clusters of the vine, and the smell of thy nose like apples; And the roof of thy mouth like the best wine for my beloved, that goeth down sweetly, causing the lips of those that are asleep to speak. (7:1-9)

The Shulamite and the Beloved have done theirs. It is now your turn to do the same thing to your spouse. Instead of the past insult, abuse, and accusation you have been bathing your spouse with, it will now be dew, rain, river, and ocean of praise. **Learn to praise than to criticize.** Bear in mind that your praise will discard inferiority complex from your spouse and make him or her believe in himself or herself.

<u>There is power in praise. The more you praise your spouse the more you win his or her love, and consequently the more your marital home becomes stronger.</u> This is how to build home with love. Conclusively, **<u>praising one's spouse is a strong winning act of love.</u>** Do this always!

Thirteen

Show Deep Love to Your Spouse

Many marital separations of wives or husbands from their spouses were caused by the fact that the wives or the husbands perceived that their spouses did no longer love them again. The same reason also accounts for many divorces.

<u>Love is a great foundation on which marriage is built and is a great pillar that holds the marriage from falling.</u> Immediately love is taking away from home, marriage has begun to fall. If this situation is not checked, in no distant time, the marriage will totally fall.

Can you please tell me the quantity of love that remains in your home? Is the love between you and your spouse increasing and fresher or decreasing and staler? It is high time you cried so that the head of your marriage will not be off. Prevention is better and easier than cure.

It is my observation that marital love in many families becomes stale and depreciates with time after their happy weddings. Broadly, as time progresses, there is a variation in marital love, which gives rise to these three stages of marriage:

   STAGE 1: honey stage
   STAGE 2: water stage
   STAGE 3: excreta stage

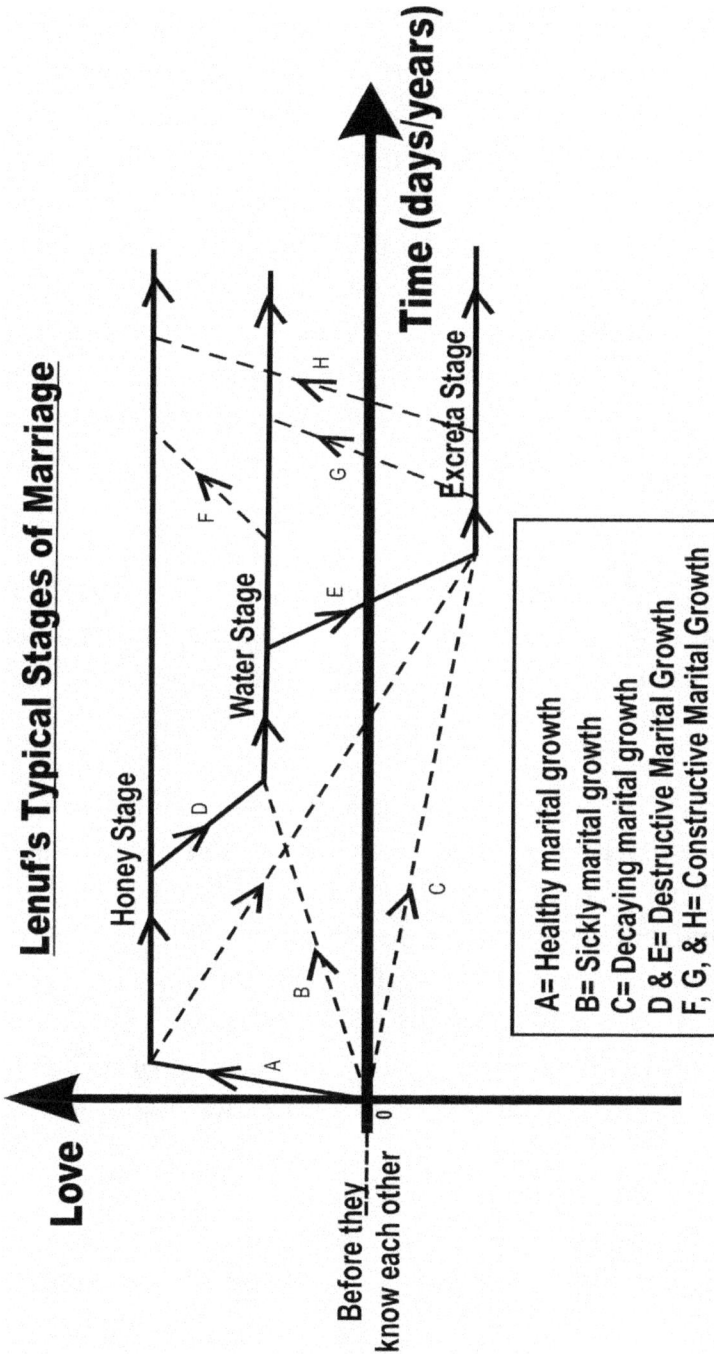

Lenuf's Typical Stages of Marriage

Love

Time (days/years)

Honey Stage

Water Stage

Excreta Stage

A

B

C

D

E

F

G

H

0

Before they
know each other

A= Healthy marital growth
B= Sickly marital growth
C= Decaying marital growth
D & E= Destructive Marital Growth
F, G, & H= Constructive Marital Growth

Before the wedding until some time after the wedding, the couple see and call each other "Honey" and many other honey-like and sweet names of loves. During this time, the marriage is very sweet. This is the honey stage of marriage. At this stage, the marital love intoxicates more than any drink in the world. Everything about this stage is sweetness – sweetness to sleep together, sweetness to stay together, sweetness to move together, sweetness to eat together, sweetness to work together and so on. The each member of the couple in this stage desires each other dearly more than honey is desire.

In some cases, short time or long time after the wedding, the marriage passes to water stage. The love the couple have for each other is just the type of natural love for water.

We take water not because it is sweet but because it is naturally necessary to be taken. At this water stage of marriage, the couple only stay together because of their children, because they do not want to have children from different fathers or different mothers, and with other reasons. At this stage, their honey love has turned to water love. At this stage, the marriage is only being endured by the couple; they are no more enjoying the union.

This second stage can continue for the rest of their lives without the first true love because of the reasons above.

However, in many cases, after much endurance, the remaining sustaining marital love of the second stage finally turns to excreta. At this time, one member of the couple sees his or her spouse as excreta or both of them see each other as excreta, irritating to each other. At this time, the couple do not want to see each other again. At this stage, they prefer separation or divorce to staying together. The marriage finally goes into divorce or separation.

In some cases, marriage starts from water stage or excreta stage. This occurs when one of the spouses is forced into such marriage. This could also be that he or she is marrying against his or her wish. (See paths B & C in the graph above).

Marriage can also rise from a worse stage to a better stage if love is brought back to the marriage (See paths F, G, &H in the graph above).

This concept discussed above is named "Lenuf Typical Stages of Marriage." The graph above illustrates this teaching explicitly.

Many marriages end up in water stage (stage 2) and some others end up in excreta stage (stage 3). Nevertheless, this is not the will of God. **The plan of God is that your marriage should start from honey stage, and remain in the**

same honey stage until death will do you and your spouse part.

My question to you is, "What stage is your marriage now?" To answer this question, call your spouse and let both of you evaluate it together.

The factor that makes marriage to migrate from honey stage to any other worse stage like water stage or excreta stage is depreciation of love in the family. Marriage begins to die when love begins to depreciate in the home. Do you now see why you must show and maintain deep undying love to your spouse throughout your lifetime? This is why I earlier said, **"Love is a great foundation on which marriage is built and is a great pillar that holds the marriage from falling."**

The marriage of the Beloved and the Shulamite is the picture of the strongest marriage that God wants in existence. The power and pillar that held the marriage throughout was love. The love was so strong that the waters of "the daughters of Jerusalem" was unable to quench it, neither did the "foxes of Solomon" was able to spoil and devour it. They never forgot to show love to each other. The commonest gift they had to offer each other was love. Hear what the Shulamite said,

*Let us get up early to the vineyards; let us
see if the vine flourish, whether the tender
grape appear, and the pomegranates bud
forth: there will I give thee my loves. The
mandrakes give a smell, and at our gates
are all manner of pleasant fruits, new and
old, which I have laid up for thee, O my
beloved. (7:12, 13)*

She told him, "There will I give thee my loves."
Do you have any love to give to your spouse? **Marital
love is more than going to bed for sexual
activity.** Those families that are in water stage still
have sex, but the true marital love for each other has
almost worn away or totally worn away.

**Marital love increases the more it is
provoked and stirred up. Learn to
provoke your spouse to love you the
more.** The Beloved and the Shulamite constantly
provoked the love of each other. Hear their statement:

Awake, O north wind; and come, thou south; blow upon my garden, that the spices thereof may flow out. Let my beloved come into his garden, and eat his pleasant fruits. (4:16)

Here, the Shulamite was provoking the love of her husband whom she referred to as "my garden." She referred to things she would use as objects of provoking and motivating the love as "wind" while she referred to his love as "spies." According to her, when the motivating ("wind") comes on him ("my garden"), his love ("spices") will flow out spontaneously. She said, "… that the spices may flow out."

When she had been highly motivated and provoked to love, she added, "Let my beloved come into his garden, and eat his pleasant fruits." She joyfully declared to him that she, "his garden," was ever ready for him. She invited him that he should come to her "his garden" to enjoy all sorts of "pleasant fruits" he desired.

As it happened in the play, it still happens today. If you can provoke the love of your spouse, he or she will totally release himself or herself to remain your spouse to the end. **Love begets love. If you want your spouse to love you, love him or her**

first. 1 John 4:19 says, *"We love Him, because He first loved us."* This is how God provoked man's love.

If the marital love of your family is depreciating or it has entered water stage, there is still much hope to resurge the love to honey stage. In what ways can this be done? This is made possible by doing things that easily provoke love. Let me give you my seven marital recommendation tips to provoke your spouse's love.

<u>Recommendation 1:</u> **To provoke your spouse's love, associate yourself with your spouse always.** As much as it is convenient and lawful, go all places with him or her. Take him or her to several places. Have a date with him or her regularly. Have your outings with him or her. Have tours with him or her. Go for picnics and other beautiful places with him or her. This constant and regular association made the family of the Beloved and the Shulamite to be very strong and to remain in honey stage throughout. Both of them were like twins. They were always seen together. I wish you could pattern your family like this.

*Come, my beloved, **let us GO** forth into the FIELD; **let us lodge** in the VILLAGES. **Let us get up early** to the VINEYARDS; **let us see** if the vine* *flourish, whether the tender grape appear,*

and the pomegranates bud forth: there

will I give thee my loves. (7:11, 12)

You can now see how they did it then. There was no place that they were unable to go together. According to the verses above, they went to "the field" together; to "the villages" together; and to "the vineyards" together. Learn to go almost everywhere with your spouse. As you do this, you are provoking him or her to love you the more.

Recommendation 2: **To provoke your spouse's love, endeavour to meet the needs of your spouse before he or she demands.** Be very watchful to know what your spouse needs at each time. Take pleasure to provide for him or her. Even if your spouse possesses all the things in the world, still go ahead to provide things for him or her as a sign of love. As a wife, learn to buy things for your spouse. The money you will use may even be his.

When you go to market, you can buy a shirt, a pair of trousers, a wrist watch or a pair of shoe and present it to your husband with words of love like, "Honey, this is what I bought to give to you who love me more than the whole world." Wives, let me reveal a secret to you. Every husband likes a caring wife greatly.

Therefore, win the love of your husband with abundant loads of care.

Likewise, husband, according to your financial ability, buy for your wife what you know or think she will value greatly. Also, according to your pocket, go for shopping with her. See how the Shulamite bountifully provided for her husband:

> *The mandrakes give a smell, and at our*
>
> *gates are all manner of pleasant fruits,*
>
> *new and old, <u>which I have laid up for thee</u>,*
>
> *O my beloved. (7:13)*

Knowing her husband's taste fully, she took pain to provide "all manner of pleasant fruits, new and old" for him. She did not ask him before she did. It was after the purchase or provision, that she invited him to see what she had for him. What great joy this created in her husband! This is provocation of love.

You too as a husband or as a wife, go and keep on surprising your spouse with your unexpected provisions. Use caring, kindness, and hospitality to provoke your spouse to love you the more.

<u>Recommendation 3:</u> **Another way of provoking your spouse to love is by**

letting your spouse to have equal access to all you enjoy. Some husbands enjoy while their

wives suffer. These husbands go to restaurants to eat delicious meals while they hardly give their wives enough money to cook quality meals at home. This attitude kills love. To provoke the love of your spouse towards you is to let him or her enjoy all you enjoy.

Let us go back to the family of the Beloved and the Shulamite and learn from them. They both enjoyed. Everything that the Beloved enjoyed or had that the Shulamite had access into and enjoyed. Hear the report of the Shulamite concerning what her husband did,

He brought me to the banqueting house,

and his banner over me was love. (2:4)

The beloved made her to have full and equal access into his "banqueting house." There are some husbands who have beverages in their own rooms and enjoy them alone while their wives lives in different rooms without any such enjoyment. This is an abnormal act in any family that does so.

In addition, let your spouse have a full access into your bank accounts and savings. Since you and your spouse are expected to be one, you can be operating the same bank account. The same bank account is only discouraged by the spouse that is two. Are you and your spouse two or one? If you are one, you should have everything in common like the early disciples in Acts 2:44-46. **Husband, let your wife know that everything you have is hers.** In addition, **let your spouse have a full access to use all you have freely without seeking your permission first.** This is one of the greatest love you can show to your spouse. Your wife should not be begging before she uses the car of the family.

Recommendation 4: **Another way of provoking your spouse to love is by shielding, supporting, and defending him or her anytime in anywhere.** This was one of the things the Beloved and his wife benefited from each other. His wife reported,

"*… and his banner over me was love.*"

(2:4)

Let your banner of support and defence be upon your spouse always. **Wrap your spouse with love. Support your spouse always. Assist him or her to do some job out of love.** Without you, he or she can easily do the job. However, use love to make it easier for him or her by joining him or her. As you do this, it will generate a fountain of love in his or her little heart, which will finally flow out to you. Do you know why? **Labour of love provokes love.** Therefore, support and assist your spouse. This is part of love.

Husbands, if you want to provoke your spouse's love really, you need to discard superstition, pride, custom, and continental (African, American, Asian etc) mentality from you. Many husbands see it as a wrong thing to assist their wives, claiming that they are the heads. Have you ever seen where labour or loads turn a human head to a foot before? Therefore, **assisting your wife, does not remove you from being her head and lord; rather it helps you to provoke her to love you than she had ever done.**

Recommendation 5: **If you want to provoke the love of your spouse, never hide any secret of yours from him or her.** Be true to him or her in every area. Show him or her everything about yourself if you believe you are one. Are you two?

When the Shulamite asked her husband to show her some facts, he did not hesitate to do this, as we can see from 1:7, 8. Try to be like this.

I made my past open wide to my spouse. She knows my mind. She knows what I do at present and what I planned to do in the future. So also, I know hers. We do not have secret from each other. This is one of the reason we love ourselves dearly.

If truly you want your spouse to love you beyond normal, never hide anything from him or her.

Recommendation 6: **Love your spouse with all your soul to provoke the latent and dormant love in him or her.** Do you know why? **Love begets love. Love kindles love. Love repairs love. Love resuscitates love. Love activates love. If you have great love for your spouse within your spirit, soul, and body, his or her love will be spontaneously provoked and sprung out in response.** Let the love you have for your spouse should not be only seen in your mouth but let it go deeper to the bottom of your soul. This is the DEEP love you are expected to show to your spouse. The Shulamite requested, "Tell me, O thou whom my soul loveth ..." (1:7)

Do you love your spouse with your soul? Can he or she read love or spell L-O-V-E in your soul? **Engage your soul to love your spouse above everything.**

Recommendation 7: **To provoke your spouse to love, fully satisfy your spouse with sexual plays of love.** Never deny or starve him or her of sexual benefits when needed. Many marriages rapidly graduate or migrate from Lenuf's Honey Stage of Marriage to Lenuf's Water Stage of Marriage and finally end up in Lenuf's Excreta Stage of Marriage due to failure of either husbands or wives to satisfy their spouses' sexual desires. While some of the spouses in water stage improvise the means of meeting their sexual desires by committing adultery with another person.

Therefore, no matter how perfectly you practise all the other principles, if you fail to satisfy your spouse's sexual desire, your marriage will definitely migrate from honey stage to any of the worse stages. This is why we should study this fact in detail. This will be done in the next chapter.

In summary, do all you know and all you can to provoke your spouse to love you more and more.

<u>Never allow your marital honey of love to degrade to excreta of hatred and consequently to divorce or marital separation.</u> Finally, <u>jealously guard your marriage with formidable pillar of love that lasts to the end.</u>

Fourteen

Satisfy Your Spouse with Plays of Love

"Stay me with flagons, COMFORT me with apples: for I am sick of love," the Shulamite pleaded. Yes, it is true that every married person always desires to be comforted and be satisfied with his or her spouse's "apples" and "flagons" content. He or she is always sick of love to be comforted with his or her spouse's "apples" and "flagons." This is why every husband must be sexually faithful to his wife, and every wife must be likewise sexually faithful to her husband.

I told you in the just concluded chapter, that failure of a spouse or both spouses to be sexually faithful caused separation or divorce (excreta stage) in marriage. It is also one of the causes why married people commit adultery. Much about this is in the HAMEO book entitled "Flee from Sexual Immorality." (Visit link http://hameo.org/HAMEOBooks.aspx in our website to order your copy).

How sexually faithful are you to your spouse? Are you not too busy that you do not have enough time for your spouse? Are you? Why are you gradually destroying your home (marriage) because of business, further education and other engagements? Let me ask you a question. What do you value most, your spouse and your family or more money, wealth, and achievement?

The Bible charges that every married person should be sexually faithful to his or her spouse. This is why God created Eve for Adam. "And the Lord God said, It is not good that the man should be alone; I will make him a help meet for him" (Genesis 2:18). This is why you must be sexually faithful to your spouse. **Marital degradation begins when a man or a woman fails to be sexually faithful to his or her spouse.** As a result, the Bible emphatically declares,

> Let the husband render to the wife due benevolence: and likewise also the wife to the husband. (1 Corinthians 7:3)

You can see from this charge that marital faithfulness is like a two-way traffic: the husband must play his part faithfully and so the wife. You, as a husband or as a wife, must ensure that you satisfactorily feed your sexually hungry spouse with plays of love. Never deny him or her. The Bible further adds,

> Defraud ye not one the other, except it be with consent for a time, that ye may give yourselves to fasting and prayer; and come together again, that Satan tempt you not for your incontinency. (1 Corinthians 7:5)

You have heard it that the Bible warns you not to defraud or deny your spouse lest Satan should use that to tempt you and degrade your home. To be forewarned is to be forearmed. Therefore, do everything under your reach to establish plays of love between you and your spouse.

A play of love is a very useful tool to win perfectly the affection of your spouse. The more you are faithful to him or her, the more he or she will love you. None of the Shulamite and the Beloved failed to play his or her part faithfully. They carried out this in various ways.

Plays of love are not static but dynamic. Plays of love are more than being on bed for sexual intercourse. They are carried out in different ways, which include kissing, hugging, embracing, caressing, sporting and playing of games, dancing and singing to each other, and many other ones you can do to satisfy your spouse. What matters here is to employ every means under your reach that can satisfy your spouse and his or her love more and more.

In the drama we are analyzing, one of the plays they involved themselves in is kissing. The Shulamite requested,

> Let him **kiss** me with the kisses of his
> mouth: for thy love is better than wine.
> (1:2)

My wife once sent me an SMS which reads, *"Love is as beautiful as two people choose to make it; it begins with a smile, grows with a kiss. Kissing is a means of getting two people so close that they cannot see anything wrong with each other. So always kiss me."*

How often do you kiss your spouse? **It is a winning act of love for you and your spouse to give a parting kiss while leaving home for work or any other place and give a welcoming kiss when you return home.** Kiss your spouse as often as possible. **Let kisses become one of your interactive languages for expressing your mind, approval, joy, appreciation, and so on.**

Let your kiss drive to the underground reservoir of love in your spouse's heart and send out a ceaseless outpouring of love that will sustain your marriage to the end. The Shulamite said,

O that thou wert as my brother, that sucked the breasts of my mother! when I

*should find thee without, I would **kiss***

thee; yea, I should not be despised. (8:1)

Another play of love between the Shulamite and the Beloved is embracing. They knew there was power in touching. **There is a latent power of marital love in sexual touching.** The Shulamite reported,

His left hand is under my head, and his

right hand doth embrace me. (2:6)

Embracing and hugging are another power tools and languages for communicating between husband and wife. **Speak out your love to your spouse with the aid of embracing and hugging. Let your spouse feel the tender love embedded in your hands. Give your spouse a never-to-be-missed patting. Pet and pat your spouse like a baby. Use patting to show your appreciation to your spouse. Embrace your spouse for every success he or she has.** Let your spouse be able to boast of your regular hogging, embracing and patting. The Shulamite boasted,

His left hand should be under my head,

and his right hand should embrace me.

Endeavour to satisfy your spouse with all plays of love you can do. There is no sin in plays of love for as long as you are legitimately married. He or she is your own sole property. As your exclusive property, every part of his or her body – from the head to the toes – is yours. The Shulamite said,

A bundle of myrrh is my well beloved

unto me; he shall lie all night betwixt my

breasts. (1:13)

As I said earlier, there are different ways of carrying out plays of love. What matter is to satisfy the sexual desire of your spouse. The play could be in terms of singing and dancing. You can beautifully compose a love-winning song to arouse your spouse's love. Whenever he or she hears the song, more love will be flowing from his or her heart to you.

Did you know that I love music well? In my family, we sing often. My wife is my music entertainer while I am hers. For instance, I composed different songs that I used to entertain my wife depending on the situation. I will show you two among the songs. The solfas of the songs are not made available in this book. However, you can get it later if you desire.

LOVE ME

Everyday of my life, only you I see.
Wher'ver I go, you are in my mind.
When I sleep, my dream about you it be;
Love me, my darling, to me be kind.

Love me, love me, darling!
Love me, love me, darling!!
Love me, love me, darling!!!
My darling, Oh!, My darling, Oh! My
darling.

Without you, I am nobody.
Goodness, Favour must be through you.
Darling, use your love clothe my body.
Love me my darling, to me be true.

In all the places where "darling" occurs in the song, you can replace the "darling" with your spouse's two-syllable name like "Mary." You can learn this song and sing it to your spouse as often as possible. The sol-fa will be made available in our website later. This is the song to make your spouse feel that he or she is somebody to you. It is also a song to arouse his or her love for you ceaselessly.

The second song is very important that I will like you to learn it also. It is a song you should use to say goodbye to your spouse when he or she is going out for anything or travelling. It is also a song to sing to his or her hearing on the telephone to tell him or her that you want him or her to come back home on time. This is the song to tell your spouse that you are "sick of love" like the Shulamite (2:5). Here it is:

I WANT TO SEE YOU

Among [a]women, I find none like you.
Your worth's more than all the [b]virgins too.
Without you, I can't be alone;
Darling, I want to see you.

> *Darling, I'm sick of your love;*
> *I want to see your face.*
> *I need, I need, I need you o;*
> *Darling, I want to see you.*

Wher'ver you go, please come back home on time;

---

[a] "women" should be replaced by "all men" if you are a wife
[b] "virgins" should be replaced by "giants" if you are a wife

You know how sick of your love I am.
Where are you please come now, now, now?
Darling, I want to see you.

Honey, I can no longer feel at home
Because I feel your great love in me
Don't cry, don't cry, don't cry, my love
Honey, I will soon be back

The stanza one and two should be sung by you while your spouse who is leaving home or not at home should reply by singing the third stanza.

Compose as many songs as possible to cheer your spouse and arouse his or her love. This is part of play of love. Let the songs be melodious with low tempo that your spouse cannot afford to do without it in any condition. Entertain your spouse with songs that will penetrate the every nook and cranny of her/his heart. Sing to your spouse the song "that goeth down sweetly, causing the lips of those that are sleep to speak" (7:9b).

In addition, send cards to each other for no reason. Send loving-winning SMS to each other. Compose poems for each other.

In summary, spend quality time to play with your spouse. **<u>Loneliness weakens and corrodes the pillar of marriage.</u>** Devise every means to keep your spouse happy. Do everything that will make your spouse prefer staying indoors with you than getting busy with other irrelevant activities outside. Never forget to give him or her kissing, hugging, embracing, patting, and and so on as often as possible. Take enough time to sport or play with your spouse as Isaac did with Rebekah his wife.

> *And it came to pass, when he had been there a long time, that Abimelech king of the Philistines looked out at a window, and saw, and, behold, Isaac was SPORTING with Rebekah his wife. (Genesis 26:8)*

Fifteen

Have Undying Passion to See & Be with Your Spouse Always

As a minister of God, I have seen many, have heard many, and have settled many disputes. I discovered that many husbands do not have passion to see and be with their wives and vice versa. My discovery also shows that many wives cannot give the accounts of the whereabouts of their husbands most times if they are asked, and vice versa. This is why many families and marriages collapse and degrade into Lenuf's Excreta Stage of Marriage.

However, this ought not to be so. For a husband or a wife to win the love of his or her spouse, he or she must have undying and unquenchable passion to always see and be with him or her. **<u>A passion for one's spouse is one of the greatest means of knowing how dearly one loves one's spouse.</u>** Immediately your spouse cannot see passion in you for him or her, he or she easily concludes within himself or herself, "My spouse does not love me dearly with all his (her) heart." As he or she keeps on ruminating on your lack of passion for him or her, his or her love for you will be gradually reducing, which will consequently degrade your marriage gradually from Lenuf's Honey Stage of Marriage.

Therefore, passion is a great winning act of love that must not be missing in your home. When I say passion for your spouse, I mean a very strong and intense feeling and desire for your spouse. Do you have a strong desire for your spouse? Do you strongly desire to see him or her when he or she is absent from home? When you are not at home, do you have a strong feeling and desire to be with him or her as soon as possible? Do you normally feel at home without him or her?

To build a strongest family or marriage, all the bricks of the marriage must be made up of passion. Again, passion is an extraordinarily abundant love that cannot be qualified and quantified.

Remember that I once told you, "Love is a great foundation on which marriage is built and is a great pillar that holds the marriage from falling." Is your marriage on the verge of falling? Quickly support it with passion.

Now, let us see how the Beloved and the Shulamite did it. Their strong marriage was an offspring of passion. Their mutual passion was so strong that they always wanted to be with each other always. The absence of one of them created imbalance and upset in the second partner. From chapter one to chapter eight of Song of Solomon, an imaginary thick line that crosses all the pages is passion. Hear what the Shulamite said,

> *I am my beloved's, and his desire is*
>
> *toward me. (7:10)*

Can't you hear her? She said, "His DESIRE is toward me." Yes, we talk about this passion. Passion, otherwise known as "strong desire" was the backbone of their marriage. According to the Shulamite, her husband had a strong desire for her always. Husbands, do you have strong desire for your wives? Do you strongly desire to see and be with your spouse always? Hear the detail of the extraordinarily abundant desire and love (i.e. passion) of the Beloved for her wife, as reported by her:

> *8 The voice of my beloved! behold, he cometh leaping upon the mountains, skipping upon the hills. My beloved is like a roe or a young hart: behold, he standeth behind our wall, he looketh forth at the windows, shewing himself through the lattice. My beloved spake, and said unto me, Rise up, my love, my fair one, and come away. For, lo, the winter is past, the rain is over and gone; The flowers appear on the earth; the time of the singing of birds is come, and the voice of the turtle is heard in our land; The fig tree putteth forth her green*

figs, and the vines with the tender grape give a good smell. <u>Arise, my love, my fair one, and come away.</u> O my dove, that art in the clefts of the rock, in the secret places of the stairs, let me see thy countenance, <u>let me hear thy voice;</u> for sweet is thy voice, and thy countenance is comely. (2:8-14)

For proper understanding, let me give further explanation especially on the underlined statements in the verses above. The Shulamite was telling us that her husband never felt at home whenever she was absent from home. The passion was always so strong that the husband would stand by the windows and start watching the way whether he could see her coming. This is what she meant when she said,

My beloved is like a roe or a young hart: behold, he standeth behind our wall, he looketh forth at the windows, shewing himself through the lattice. (2:9)

Husbands, can you see a great strong desire or passion for one's spouse? Wives, can you also see it? Can your husband or wife testify to your undying desire to see him or her whenever he or she is absent from home?

In addition, at times, he sent messages to her to suspend every other activity she had and rush back home. He easily sent anybody he saw going to where she was to tell her to return home quickly. His message is found in verse 10 and 13. His message to her is:

Rise up, my love, my fair one, and come

away.

If there were telegraphs or telephones then, his message to his wife on the phone would be, "Arise, my love, my fair one, and come away." Do you have even any desire to see your spouse let alone of telephoning him or her to come back home on time? Are you not a type of spouse that says, "Any day he (she) likes, let him (her) come back home from his (her) journey"? Do you have any desire to know the welfare of your spouse whether he or she arrives safely to where he or she travels?

Passion strengthens marriage. As the Beloved was so passionate to see his wife always, so must you do. The Beloved was always very desirous to see the countenance (i.e. the face) of his wife and to hear her voice speaking. He said,

"O my dove, that art in the clefts of the

rock, in the secret places of the stairs, let

me see thy countenance, let me hear thy

voice; for sweet is thy voice, and thy

countenance is comely. (2:14)

Do you have the same desire to see your spouse always? Do you have a strong passion to hear his or her voice whenever he or she is not with you? Do you strongly desire to see him or her over and over? In the case of the Beloved, he sent messages to her,

Arise... come away ... Let me see thy

countenance, let me hear thy voice...

(2:13,14)

If there is anything I greatly desire to see every time, it is the face of my wife. The second song entitled "I Want to See You" I gave to you in the just concluded chapter was composed as a result of great thirst and passion to see whom I planned to marry when I was still a bachelor. As I was in a certain place, I desired to see her but I was unable. The next thing that followed was that I started singing to see her:

"Darling, I'm sick of your love;
I want to see your face.
I need, I need, I need you o;
Darling, I want to see you."

When I sang it, I put her name instead of "darling" in the song. The song was just a product of passion.

My soul is so much cleaved and tied to my wife's soul that I cannot do without her. As the Shulamite did, I like to see my wife and hear her voice always. This is the secret of any strong marriage. You and your spouse should be like the Shulamite and the Beloved that always urged each other to return home on time. Their statement to each other from the mouth of the Shulamite is:

> *Make haste, my beloved, and be thou like*
>
> *to a roe or to a young hart upon the*
>
> *mountains of spices. (8:14)*

Therefore, have an undying passion to see and be with your spouse always. Build a strong desire for your spouse in your heart. This was a unique characteristic of the Beloved's family. Whenever they were not together, they were not having perfect rest of mind. They found it difficult to sleep alone individually. The Shulamite testified,

> *By night on my bed I sought him whom*
>
> *my soul loveth: I sought him, but I found*

him not. I will rise now, and go about the city in the streets, and in the broad ways I will seek him whom my soul loveth: I sought him, but I found him not. (3:1,2)

Can you see the level of their mutual passion and interdependence? Their sleep was not sweet whenever they were not together. This is as a result of power of love. How passionate are you towards your spouse? It is a sad thing for me to hear or see a husband living in a separate room from his wife. This was never done by the Shulamite and the Beloved.

If you want your marriage to be strong, you must come and learn from the Beloved and the Shulamite. There is a lot to learn from them. You need a passion for your spouse as they did. Neither of them was able to sleep whenever his or her partner failed to come home as scheduled. You too go and develop an undying passion for your spouse. Let your soul be tied to his or hers.

Another thing I see about the passions of the Beloved and the Shulamite for each other is their ability to give the account of the whereabouts of each other. Each one of them could easily tell where his or her spouse was or went. There was a time that the daughters of Jerusalem asked the Shulamite about the whereabouts of her husband and she answered well. Here it is:

The Daughters of Jerusalem

> *Whither is thy beloved gone, O thou fairest among*
>
> *women? whither is thy beloved turned aside? that we*
>
> *may seek him with thee. (6:1)*

The Shulamite

> *My beloved is gone down into his garden, to the beds*
>
> *of spices, to feed in the gardens, and to gather*
>
> *lilies.(6:2)*

It is a sad thing in many families nowadays that many a husband cannot tell the whereabouts of his wife and many a wife cannot tell the whereabouts of her husband. It is a shameful thing. Please, do not be offended because of my question. You, a husband or a wife, can you prove to me the whereabouts of your spouse at each time? I think what you know about your spouse is that he or she is not at home now or he or she has come back. However, can you tell where he or she is now or where he or she went? This was not so in the Beloved's family.

Moreover, I also observed that many husbands or wives leave home anyhow without informing their spouses concerning their movements. This is what a woman reported to me concerning her husband sometimes ago. Is that good? No! **Please and**

please, be passionate to know the whereabouts of your spouse. In addition, be passionate to tell your spouse about your whereabouts.

Never be separated from your spouse. **Physical separation is the beginning of and foundation for marital separation.** Therefore, do not allow quest for money, business engagement, and acquisition of further knowledge in education to separate you from your spouse. Have undying passion to live with and see your spouse. Make yourself to be closer to your spouse than ever. Do not be too far from him or her.

Marriage or family degrades from Lenuf's Honey Stage of Marriage to Water Stage or Excreta Stage as passion reduces between husband and wife. Divorce, separation, fighting, and adultery crawl into marriage as passion and love are withdrawn from the home. Therefore, do not allow business, quest for wealth, education, and other engagements to reduce your passion for your spouse. Take your spouse more important than any other things in life. Take your spouse as the best treasure you can ever acquire. Be careful not to lose him or her.

Finally, **set your spouse in the centre of your heart to the extent that you cannot do without thinking about him or her.** Here is the heart's request of your spouse to you as now onwards:

> *Set me as a seal upon thine heart, as a seal*
>
> *upon thine arm... (8:6)*

Sixteen

Reference Your Spouse with Evaluated Love-Winning Names

You have been taught many things that will enhance the stability of your home in the just concluded chapter. Now, we are moving toward the end of this book. With all you have been taught so far, how do you currently evaluate your spouse? Have you started evaluating him or her than you ever did? Now, **transform your evaluations concerning your spouse into names that you will be using to reference or call him or her.** These names will go a long way to win his or her love for you more and more.

I observed that some husbands and wives try to be rude in the ways they reference their spouses. For instance, a young lady at 22 years, who is a wife to an old man of 50 years of age, will prefer to call the man his name, let say James, than calling him "darling," "my love," "daddy" etc.

Even, if you are older than your spouse is with many years, still find means of reverencing him or her respectfully and honourably. As your spouse begins to sense rudeness in you, his or her affection for you begins to reduce.

There is a certain man I know well. He uses about 17 years to be older than his wife is. Nevertheless, one thing is challenging in this man. He always references his wife honourably. Besides, he does not only call her an honourable name but he also respects her in his speech. When his wife returns from work or any other place, he does not say, "You are welcome," but "You are welcome, ma." Despite he is far older, yet he respects her. This is a lesson for you.

I have observed that many wives lack good manners, so also many husbands. If you have not been reverencing and honouring your spouse, it is high time you started. Respect begets respect. **<u>Love of one's spouse is easily won when there is respect than when it is lacking.</u>**

One of the things that strengthened the marriage of the Shulamite and the Beloved in spite of all adversities and oppositions, is their mutual respect for one another. They never abuse or insult each other once. From chapter one to the last chapter of Song of Solomon, there is no single verse where you can hear or see either of them calling his or her spouse by his or her real name before the whole public.

How did they call or what did they call each other? They called each other with high respect and honour. All the names each called his or her spouse was given because of his or her thoughtful evaluations of the worth of his or her spouse. Besides, all the names are love-winning names. The following ten names were what they called each other:

- **My Love** –   1:9,15; 2:10,13; 4:17; 5:2; 6:4; 7:6
- **My Beloved** – 1:14,16; 2:3,8,9,10,16; 4:16;
                   5:2,4,6,8,10,16; 6:2,3; 7:10,11,13; 13;
                   8:14
- **My Well-beloved** – 1:13
- **My Spouse** – 4:8,9,10,11,12; 5:1
- **My Sister** – 4:9,10,12; 5:1,2
- **My Friend** – 5:16
- **My Fair One** – 2:10,13
- **My Garden** – 5:1; 4:12,16
- **My Undefiled** – 5:2; 6:9
- **My Dove** – 2:14; 5:2; 6:9

These are the carefully selected and thoughtfully evaluated love-winning names that held the Shulamite's marriage firmly to the end. These served different purposes to them. As a result, let me group the names into three groups for proper analysis.

Group 1 Names are the names they used to express their **AFFECTION AND PASSION** for each other. These are
- "My Love,"
- "My Beloved," and
- "My Well-beloved."

These names are indirect means of telling each other "I love you so much." Can you now see how thoughtful they were before they called each other? They called each other out of evaluation.

Group 2 Names are the names they used to express the **CORDIALITY OF THEIR RELATIONSHIP.** These names are
- "My Spouse,"
- "My Sister," and
- "My Friend."

Any of these were used depending on their moods. For instance, the Beloved referred to the Shulamite as "My Sister." This he did to express how dear she was to him. Within him, his speech is, "This is my flesh and my bone." This is my blood. This sister is mine, even the blood sister whom I must care for with all my life.

At times, he called her, "My Spouse." That is, this is the mother or will be the mother of all my children. This is my wife who cares for me in every area. While the Shulamite referred to her husband as "My Friend." She saw her husband as the greatest friend to have in life. A friend in need is a friend indeed. Within her, "This is the person who accepted me as I was. He did not despise me despite I was black. This is nothing or nobody but my friend indeed." Can you see thoughtful evaluated names?

Group 3 Names are the names they used to express each other's **BEAUTY AND UNIQUENESS**. The names are
- "My Fair One,"
- "My Undefiled,"

- "My Garden," and
- "My Dove."

They used these names to tell each other, "My spouse you are very pretty and fine. There is no one like you. There is no single spot of ugliness and abnormality in you." 4:7 affirms, "<u>Thou art all fair</u>, my love; there is NO SPOT in thee." Each time anyone of them heard his or her spouse calling him or her any of these names, he was very happy that his or her spouse appreciated his or her beauty and uniqueness.

When each of them called, "My undefiled," he or she was referring to the spotlessness of his or her spouse. This is uniqueness. In addition, when "My Garden" was called, the caller meant the beauty of his or her spouse. I hope you know how beautiful, attractive, useful, and fruitful a garden is!

They used "My Dove" to show extraordinary, attractive, unique, and humble (or respectful) each of the spouses was. 2:14 says, "O <u>my dove</u>, that art in the clefts of the rock, in the secret places of the stairs, let me see thy countenance, let me hear thy voice..." This verse talks about the uniqueness and attractiveness of the dove, a metaphor for his spouse. Again, dove is a gentle and harmless bird (Matthew 10:16). Therefore, he used "my dove" to refer to the respectful, harmless, and humble lifestyle of his spouse.

Again, 6:9 says, "<u>My dove</u>, my undefiled is but

one; she is the only one of her mother, she is the choice one of her that bare her…" This verse talks about the uniqueness of his spouse as a dove. He showed to his wife, "Darling you are not abnormal but highly unique like a dove among all other birds. In fact, you are my one and only." In the verse, he said, "My dove…is but one…she is the choice one…" That is, the Shulamite was ONE AND ONLY.

Coming to you as a married person, how do you see your spouse? What do you call your spouse? Do you have any love-winning name for you spouse? You too can emulate the Beloved and the Shulamite today. They called each other not less than ten (10) love-winning names after thoughtful evaluation of each other's worth. This is why their marriage remains a model for lovers of successful marriage to pattern their marriages after. They never called each other contemptible names but respectful and honourable names.

Today, many names exist at your disposal with which you can reference your spouse. Like the Shulamite's family, you can call your spouse, "My Love," "My Dove," "My Sister (or Brother)," "My Friend," "My Spouse or My Wife or My Husband or My Owner or My lord (as Sarah did, meaning my master or my owner)," "My Beloved," "My Well-beloved," "My Fair One," and so on. In addition, you can use those commonest names you hear around you like "Honey," "Darling," "One and Only," "My Darling Love," "Daddy," "Mummy," "Sweetheart," "My Dear or MD,"

"Mine," and so on. You can also put "my" before your spouse name, e.g. "My Mary."

As you call your spouse, study to know the names that he or she loves most. Then call him or her those favourite names of his or hers always. Be thoughtful on the type of names to use. Call your spouse according to your rating and evaluation of who he or she is to you or according to his or her worth. At any time, I may choose to call my wife, "My hope," "My life," "My teacher," and so on. Each name serves different purpose.

The name you call your spouse can go a long way to increase his or her love for you. Therefore, call him or her with full reverence. This is what Sarah did and we are enjoined to follow her footsteps:

> *Even as Sara obeyed Abraham,* **calling him lord**: *whose daughters ye are, as long as ye do well, and are not afraid with any amazement. Likewise, ye husbands, dwell with them according to knowledge, giving honor to the wife, as to the weaker vessel, and as being heirs together of the grace of life; that your prayers be not hindered. (1 Peter 3:6, 7)*

<u>Wife, honour your husband; husband, honour your wife; Call each other with full respect</u>. Imitate the Shulamite

and the Beloved. **Use your mouth to pull out the heart and the soul of your spouse and tie them to yours through the names you call him or her. A thoughtful evaluated name is a mighty winning tool of love in marriage.**

Part F

THE CONCLUSIVE THEME OF THE DRAMA

Seventeen

The Power of Love

The power of love is the theme of the whole drama. When enticement, oppositions, belittling, and other forces from King Solomon and his ministers, the daughters of Jerusalem combined to pull down the marriage between the Shulamite and her beloved, the dormant resistive power of love was seen in action. The more Solomon and his people tried, the more the mutual · love between the Shulamite and her spouse resisted the "foxes." When Solomon discovered that nothing could break their mutual love, the theme of the drama was therefore echoed:

> *... for love is strong as death; jealousy*
>
> *is cruel as the grave: the coals thereof are*
>
> *coals of fire, which hath a most vehement*
>
> *flame. **Many waters cannot quench***
>
> ***love, neither can the floods drown it***:
>
> *if a man would give all the substance of*
>
> *his house for love, it would utterly be*
>
> *contemned. (8:6, 7)*

Yes, this is the power of love. **Love has** **power to fight all forces that militate** **against marriage and at the same, to hold** **it from falling.** This is why love must not be lacking in any marriage. "For love is strong as death." **Love is stronger than the strongest man on earth is. Death can kill the strongest man but cannot kill love.** Why? This is because love itself is as strong as death. Since love is not weaker than death, the latter has no power over it. This is why **death can only part a couple but cannot kill their love for each other even after death.**

There is incomparable power in love. As death has power over every human being, so also love has power over every couple to bind them together in love and sustain their marriage from falling if they permit HIM in their home.

Love is so strong and powerful that nothing in this life can conquer it. Even, "many waters cannot quench love, neither can the floods drown it" (8:7a) Since love is the strongest, with love in any family, there will be no need to fear all the attempts of the enemies to dissolve the marriage. Every force that combats marriage is under the foot of love. If you and your spouse permit love in your family, all the opposing forces against your marriage will be trampled to pieces under the foot of the same love.

Again, love is so powerful that nothing can entice or change it. This is because "if a man would give all the substance of his house for love, it would utterly be contemned" (8:7b). Solomon tried and used all his substances and wealth to influence and entice the Shulamite but he was unable to win her love due to the unlimited love she had for her lover, the beloved. The verses below give the record of some of the substances that Solomon used to influence the Shulamite.

> *Solomon had a vineyard at Baalhamon; he let out the vineyard unto keepers; every one for the fruit thereof was to bring a thousand pieces of silver. My vineyard, which is mine, is before me: thou, O Solomon, must have a thousand, and those that keep the fruit thereof two hundred. Thou that dwellest in the gardens, the companions hearken to thy voice: cause me to hear it. (8:11-13)*

Can't you see how wealthy Solomon was? From the verse, he had a great vineyard. What a large substance and possession to influence the Shulamite! Besides, he had many keepers who served as lessees that maintained the vineyard. Each one of them delivered money worth of "a thousand pieces of silver" for the lease to Solomon on a regular basis. Let us say the keepers were at least one thousand in number. Therefore, in every month or term, they delivered one million pieces of silver of money to him. What a huge amount of money!

Remember that Solomon had many other investments and many great people from which he got unlimited wealth (1 Kings 10:22-29). This is a golden king that used gold for almost everything including his cups (1 Kings 10:21, 14-20).

In the verses quoted above, each keeper of the vineyard may have "two hundred" on a regular basis. As a result, these keepers were richer than many rich men around. These keepers were so rich that people admired them and listened to them. Women were ready to marry them easily without any prior plea due to this wealth. This is why verse 13 above says,

> *Thou that dwellest in the gardens, the*
>
> *companions hearken to thy voice: cause*
>
> *me to hear it.*

Each of these keepers, "that dwellest in the gardens" received just only two hundred and became so influential in the society that "the companion hearken to" his "voice." He was so influential that every woman was ready to marry him. How enthusiastic do you think all women would be running after Solomon their master who had unlimited wealth. It is no wonder that 1000 women willingly married him (1 Kings 11:3).

Since every woman was running after him and the keepers of his vineyard, Solomon also believed that the Shulamite would be easily influenced by all these things. Solomon came to her and said, "I am King Solomon, the greatest king, the wisest man, and the richest man on earth. I want to marry you, o girl. I'll do for you whatever you want. I will take you to another level of your life. Is that all right by you?" Her usual reply was,

> *I am my beloved's, and his desire is*
>
> *toward me. (7:10)*

When Solomon discovered that she was not impressed at all, he raised a committee of women known as "the daughters of Jerusalem" whom he thought would help him to convince her. He even furnished apartments for them in the State House or palace of chariot (3:9, 10). All these people tried all they could but she turned down their offers by saying,

> *I charge you, O daughters of Jerusalem,*
>
> *that ye stir not up, nor awake my love,*
>
> *until he please. (8:4)*

Solomon used all his resources and substances to win her but she made him to know, "All these things do not impress me at all." Solomon then found out why none of all his resources and substances impressed her at all. He later discovered that she so much loved the Beloved. Solomon then tried to break the love but he was unable. All his substances failed him. This is why, it was then written,

> *If a man would give <u>all the substance</u> of*
>
> *his house for love, it would utterly be*
>
> *contemned. (8:7b)*

"All the substance of his (Solomon's) house" was "utterly contemned" before the love the Shulamite had for her spouse. Solomon therefore realized that "love is strong as death; jealousy is cruel as the grave: the coals thereof are coals of fire, which hath a most vehement flame" (8:6b). Solomon finally withdrew when he discovered that there was unlimited power in love. Truly, there is power in love.

> *Many waters cannot quench love, neither*
>
> *can the floods drown it. (8:7a)*

The central truth or the theme of the whole drama is "The Power of Love." If you can allow love to saturate your home thoroughly, you will also discover this unlimited power of love. **There is nothing can quench, conquer, destroy, eliminate, and entice love. Love supersedes every force around it.** There are no "little foxes" that can devour love. Let love reign in your family.

Bring love into your family so that people around will be able to witness the unlimited power of love. Go, renew, and increase your love for your spouse in order to be able to withstand all "the daughters of Jerusalem" that may come your way. For you to enjoy your marriage to the end, the love of your spouse must never depart from your heart. Take your spouse as he or she is and develop him or her to your taste. As you have learnt in all the earlier chapters, play your part by doing all you can to win all the love of your spouse.

Above all that you have learnt in this book, let the love of your spouse be in your heart always. Both of you must serve God together. As you serve, God will be increasing the love. To get the love more abundantly, pray to God, "O give me more love for my husband (or wife), to love him (or her) with all my life." Also, pray to God to make your spouse love you more and more on the daily basis.

The more love you have in your family, the more power you and your

spouse have to remain a couple to the end. There is unlimited power in love. **A happy marriage or home is the product of the power of love.** Do you need a happy home? If your answer is "Yes," you need love first. This love comes from God. **You therefore need sound relationship with God in order to maintain a sound relationship with your spouse.**

Do all you can to make your spouse love you more and more? Never grieve your spouse; be prompt to his or her request; respect him or her; praise him or her always; never be ashamed of him or her but be proud of him or her; call him or her the names of love that he or she cherishes greatly. Satisfy him or her with plays of love; give him or her worthy supports always; never hide any secret from him or her. Let your spouse have access to all you enjoy; have a passion to see and be with your spouse always; provoke him or her to love you greatly by loving him or her with all your soul; and always involve God through prayer to take away and deal with all the "little foxes" that militate against your marriage.

As you do all these faithfully, your home will become a home of love that will stand against every force and opposition. **Never allow God to be**

<u>missing in your family. God is the foundation of true love, while true love is the foundation of happy home or marriage.</u> As you do this, people will witness the power of love in your family and testify to the power of love in your family. You and your spouse should come together and rebuild love in your home.

Let your daily message to your spouse be "Set me as a seal upon thine heart, as a seal upon thine arm: for love *is* strong as death" (8:6a). You must not only tell this but you must put this in practice. Set your spouse as a seal upon your heart wherever you go. As you do this, if anybody wants to write a story of your family, he will discover the theme of your home to be:

> *Many waters cannot quench love, neither*
>
> *can the floods drown it: if a man would*
>
> *give all the substance of his house for love,*
>
> *it would utterly be contemned. (8:7)*

I will draw down the curtain here. You are welcome to the end of this course in Lenuf University of King Solomon (LUKS). I believe you can now fully manage your Marriage or Courtship now, having successfully gone through the Marriage & Courtship Management course in LUKS. See you and take care of your spouse greatly until we meet again. God bless you. Amen.

ABOUT HAMEO
(GOD'S PEOPLE AT GOD'S WORK)

Holiness A Must Evangelistic Outreach (HAMEO) is a God-instituted body of Christ with a God-given mandate and commission to reach the world, especially the Gospel-poorly-reached areas and countries with holiness-centred messages, crusades, outreaches, evangelisms, seminars, literatures, and other God-led means.

Holiness A Must Evangelistic Outreach (HAMEO) is a holiness-focused missionary group. HAMEO was commissioned to preach the total holiness demanded by God – from the first word of the Holy Bible, i.e. "IN" to the last word, i.e. "AMEN" (Genesis to Revelation). As a result, "We preach nothing but the whole Scripture, Jesus, and His Sanctifying Mission."

Feel free to contact us anytime through:
* www.hameo.org;   * Godspeople@hameo.org

Follow us on Twitter at www.twitter.com/hameopeople. Be our fan in Facebook at www.facebook.com/hameopeople. These links are also available on the home page of our website.

How current are you with ELB Explorer? This is our online publication for touching general life's issues through the truth of the Scriptures. This is published in our website. It also mailed freely to subscribers. Just visit http://hameo.org/ELBEXPLORER.aspx and subscribe for yourself and other loved ones.

You can also submit your Gospel write-ups to gpt@hameo.org to be published under our **Gospel Article** page in our website for others to learn from you. Check http://hameo.org/HAMEOBooks.aspx for other HAMEO inspiring books.

HAMEO…*we preach nothing but the whole Scripture, Jesus, and His Sanctifying Mission!*

THE AUTHOR

L. U. Eninobor (Pastor Lenuf) is a God's ordained minister and missionary to reach nations, especially those with "low transactions" in terms of godliness, with Christ's Gospel messages of salvation from sin, and holiness of heart to God. He is a coordinating leader of Holiness A Must Evangelistic Outreach (HAMEO) under the directorship of the Almighty God, the Sender. He lives happily with his wife, Mary (Pastor Mary E) and they are blessed with twins - Louis and Louisa.

www.ingramcontent.com/pod-product-compliance
Lightning Source LLC
Chambersburg PA
CBHW071429090426
42737CB00011B/1606